DESTINY HIDDEN IN DARK PLACES

Muyiwa Olumoroti

Elder Babs Oludimu

Dr Muyiwa Olumoroti
12/4/2011

WORD2PRINT
A division of One-Touch UK

First published in the United Kingdom in 2011
by Word2Print
www.word2print.com
info@word2print.com; info@profsexperts.com

ISBN 978-1-908588-00-5

Produced by
The Choir Press, Gloucester

Contents

Appreciation

First of all I must thank God Almighty who put the idea for this book in my spirit and who made it possible for me to complete it despite all the pressures and doubts. I will forever be indebted to many men and women who have assisted with reading drafts at every stage. I wish to acknowledge the assistance I received from Helen Valdes, Kemi Oyesola, Onike Ijete and Patricia Olowu. You have contributed immensely to the preparation of this book and you are all to me 'helpers of destiny'. I am grateful to Dr Tayo Adeyemi who has granted me permission to use extracts from some of his sermon notes, and for continuing to pour his life into many over the years. He has given me the reason to continue to believe that anything is possible in God if you set your mind to it.

Writing a book necessarily bites into one's family time and my wife Kemi, and children – Wonu, Tomisin and Anjola – have been extremely understanding and supportive. You have been with me through thick and thin – you are very much loved and highly appreciated.

I also wish to acknowledge the skilful assistance that I received from the staff of Word2Print Publishing and Miles Bailey of The Choir Press in the final production of this book. I thank you all.

> Now to Him who is able to do exceedingly abundantly above all that we ask or think, according to the power that works in us, to Him be glory in the church by Christ Jesus to all generations, forever and ever. Amen.

Ephesians 3:20–21 (New King James Version)

Destiny Hidden in Dark Places will make you think, laugh and cry. This book will also help you to appreciate what you have, and most importantly, it will help you to keep the right perspectives as you go through the ups and downs of life. It is time to bounce back!

Preface

'Life is funny', and it is true, not only because of the challenges we face from time to time, but due to the pain we feel and the mystery or the drama that sometimes surrounds us when we find ourselves in places or situations where we would rather not be. Life itself is a race; and we go through the highs and the lows, the tops of mountains and the depth of valleys where there may be darkness. It is when we face dark periods in our lives that we often ask the questions – what, who, where, why, when, and how. That's also the time when people are most likely to ask the ultimate questions: Does God exist? Does He love me? Where is God when all these things are happening or where is God in all this? Questions like these are usually asked when people find themselves in darkness.

Challenges are part and parcel of life, whether you or others cause them. Some are sudden, others happen over time, but none of us like them. Naturally when you are in the dark, you want to come out, and in that process may act irrationally or even foolishly, blame others or God, and doubt His love for you. We all forget that good things can come out of bad situations and that destiny can be hidden in dark places.

The writing of this book has been inspired by God through the ordeal of the Chilean miners in the summer of 2010, and the ordeal of men and women before and after them. God is unchangeable; He cannot and will not change. You will learn one or two things about dark places in this book; and what to do and what not to do when you find yourself in an unwelcome and very difficult situation. You will also read about what God does with darkness in people's lives. The testimonies of people who have been through difficulties in their lives will also encourage you.

Destiny, you must believe, can come out of dark places. My prayer is that as you read this book, whether you have passed, or are passing through a dark place right now or not, you will be ministered to in a very special way. God Himself will receive all the glory, honour and praise. Your life will never remain the same again.

1

In The Dark

Only a bat likes to be in the dark, and no one in his right mind would like to be in darkness particularly if they can afford not to be. I recently read about *ambergris* – the precious essential ingredient used to make good and expensive perfumes. It is found inside sperm whales' intestines, a very murky and dark place. Have you ever wondered why men go into dark and deep mines? The places in the Earth full of coal, oil, gold, diamonds and other precious metals are not located in the back garden where they can be easily reached. You have to look deep down, and many times beneath hard rocks. Treasures are hidden in dark places; and the same is true for destiny.

On 5 July 2010, news broke worldwide of the plight of 33 Chilean miners who were trapped over half a mile below the surface of the ground. Part of the San José copper and gold mine near Copiapó, Chile had collapsed, with 700,000 tonnes of rock sealing off the lower third of the mine. These ordinary men had gone about their normal business to earn a living to provide for their families. One of the men, 27-year-old Carlos Bugueno, was on his first shift when he became trapped. For a reason which may not have been the miners' fault, they were all thrown into perpetual darkness with little hope of survival before they made contact with the surface on the 17th day of their 69-day ordeal. These men did not want to be there and in fact did not plan to be there but had to wait there until they were rescued.

I followed the news daily with free newspapers which I picked up on my way to and from work. I was sure in my spirit that somebody somewhere was already preparing to buy rights to the miners' story – to make a drama of some sort, publish it as a best-seller or send it to Hollywood for the next blockbuster. I predicted that when these men came to the surface, their lives would never be the same again, and that for many of them, God would turn their disaster into destiny, and their situation into stardom.

One day, I heard God say clearly in my spirit: *"You are right; I am the God that can turn any situation around. I know that you know what I can do but many people who are going through dark periods or difficult situations in their lives do not know what you know."* I heard God ask me a question: *"What are you going to do about this story which you have been following up for two months?"* I said: *"Nothing – the news media are reporting the story and I have said prayers for the miners. There is nothing else for me to do. You are the God who has the solution in your hand, not me."* I gave God the perfect answer and forgot about it.

As the rescue of the Chilean miners drew nearer, I became increasingly fixated with the news. I was sure the miners would be out in days unless something went disastrously wrong. I was completely taken in by the stories and the events that were unfolding – the drama, panic, anxieties, disappointments, uncer-tainties and even the news of adultery that came to light during the miners' ordeal. Watching the build-up to the rescue mission was gripping and at the same time painful for the miners' families and their admirers around the world. I wondered what was going on in the minds of the miners and their families.

On 7 October 2010, a week before the miners were rescued, God again said quietly in my spirit: *"I am the one that can turn any situation around. The miners are coming out of their dark places."* I knew that already and I said: *"I knew that, God, I thought we were both clear about that."* God then said to me: *"Write about destiny hidden in dark places, and I want you to take a study in darkness."* I didn't expect that! I said to myself: "I *think God is being presumptuous here. The miners have not even been rescued yet."*

I have learnt to be honest to myself, and I try to obey the voice of God when He is saying something. I heard Him clearly; this was no ordinary voice; it was the voice of God impinging on my spirit. Writing about darkness was something I initially found difficult to do. I asked myself several times: *"Where on Earth would I get materials to write about darkness, with all that has been written already?"* How would I approach anyone – my friends or mentors – and tell them: *"I want you to help me, I want to study darkness?"* I thought even people that knew me well would probably first think I had joined a dark society of some sort. However the urge to write about how God is able to bring people out of dark places did not leave me even though I tried to shrug it off. I took a leap of faith and began to write.

As I began to write, I heard on 19 November 2010 that another 29 miners were trapped at the Pike River mine outside the town of Greymouth, New Zealand. One of the miners was a 17-year-old man on his first shift. A series of huge explosions had sealed the men's fate and highly toxic gases from the mines prevented a rescue operation for many days. Those 29 miners did not come out alive like the Chilean miners. Their bodies could not be brought to the surface for many months and on 17 January 2011, it was confirmed that recovery of the bodies was unlikely. The miners' families had to live with the possibility that the bodies of their loved ones may never be retrieved. It was, and still is, a very dark situation.

I was discouraged by the story of the New Zealand miners and felt "What's the point?". It was the complete opposite of what had happened to the Chilean miners – the event that set me on course for this writing exercise. I have no explanation for the tragic event of the New Zealand miners but I knew this event did not change God one bit. I can confidently say that even in the dark hours which the families of the New Zealand miners found themselves in, God was at work. He had already begun to work on their behalf, whether the families can see it or not. I knew very clearly that the plan of God is always to do them good, and to give all of them a great future even though it might be difficult to understand or explain. God can turn any darkness into destiny. I decided to continue to write no matter what.

Destiny speaks about destination and the plan that God has for you in any particular situation. According to the Bible, the outcome of that plan is good (Jeremiah 29:11). Despite this assurance, sometimes you may find yourself in difficulties, adverse situations or circumstances which I refer to as darkness throughout this book. This darkness is what might be attempting to negate the word of God over your life. However, no matter what a bad situation looks like, the outcome in God's mind for you is for you to come out victorious.

Whenever you are reaching for a goal and it appears your view is being obscured by events or your stretch is being hindered by known and unknown forces, be sure that God's intention is for you to attain what He had already predestined for you. I dare say boldly that if you find yourself in a situation in which you are completely trapped, your destiny in God is to come out to declare His glory. Your true destiny is in God's plans and though it may appear to be hidden inside dark periods in your life, it will not change no matter how dark the situation is. The different shades of darkness can never ever abort the eternal plans of the Almighty.

2

The Shades Of The Dark

———————

Dark places come in various shades, magnitudes and shapes. Yours may not be the same as mine but all of us sometimes face difficult situations in life. For some it may be easy and for others very hard. It may be a natural disaster that is threatening a person's existence; or the challenge may be unemployment, barrenness, illness or marital difficulties. These are all dark situations and no one likes them. A dark place is when the bills are piling up, and the creditors are calling but your income is dwindling. It is the place where you are when you invited people for a housewarming two years ago and today the house is being repossessed. A dark place is where your relationship or marriage collapses right in front of you and you can't really do anything about it. It is the place where you are when you have lost a loved one – young, middle-aged or elderly.

A dark place is where you are when your 15-year-old daughter leaves home, and you are not sure whether she is sleeping on the bench in the park, in the bus garage, a train station or on someone's chest in the middle of nowhere. You are not sure if she has run away with an older man to a far-flung place or whether she is on heroin or cocaine. A dark place is where you are when your phone rings and brings you the hope that your 17-year-old son might come back home only for your hope to be dashed again. You hear that he has been injured in an accident but rather than come home, he decides to stay with his friends who are hooked on sex, gambling and drugs.

A dark place is when the woman who you have been waiting for calls off the wedding and goes off with another man. You find out later that her family thought she would be better off with Mr Jones who is richer, and who has the prospect of offering her and them a better life. A lady is in a dark place when after she was engaged to the love of her life, the man decides to travel to a far place and never returns. The pasture on the other side became too green and he decided to settle with another woman. A man might equally find himself in a dark place after finding a woman he loves, uses all his life savings to improve her qualifications for better job prospects, only to find out that his wife-to-be has found another man in college who speaks better English than he does, and is already carrying a child for the other man.

You may have been married for five or seven years with no child and the doctors have said there is nothing more they can do. Your mother-in-law who hitherto understood the difficulties is now encouraging her son not to put all his eggs in one basket. You are a Christian and he loves the Lord, but does not know what to do. That is a very dark place indeed.

A dark place is when the man of your dreams turned you into a punchbag; abused, misused and battered you, and then left you for another woman. To make it worse, he not only left you with bruises and wounds to nurse, he left you with huge debts in both your names. You look for a new phrase to use every time the children ask: "Where is daddy?" The bailiffs keep on returning and you don't know what to do. As the clock ticks, you have nowhere to go. You are definitely in a dark and difficult situation.

A man or woman is in a very dark place when after they have used their life savings or taken out a huge loan for an investment – either for import and export, commercial dairy or fish farming, or massive crop production or a transport business – all of a sudden there is political turmoil, economic recession, policy changes, drought, outbreak of diseases or scarcities that bring their dream to an abrupt end. There is nothing to show for the massive investment; the creditors are calling and the loans still have to be repaid. They sold their only house in the hope that the economy would get better but rather than things improving they are getting worse. The next thing – they wish they had never been born. That is a person in darkness.

You find yourself in a difficult situation when you hear for the tenth time in a year the infamous phrase: "I'm sorry to let you know you did not get the job." A dark place is where you are when you go into business with someone you call a friend with all of your life savings and borrowed money, only for the business to collapse and for your friend to disappear into thin air. You are in a dark place when you have worked for twenty years and seem not to be going anywhere. You have been repeatedly passed over for promotion and the people you trained with on the job are now your bosses. You are told the problem is either with the way you dress, people's skills, your management style, efficiency or even your accent.

You are in a dark place when you don't know where the next meal is going to come from. The bowls are dry and you have to borrow money to buy the next formula feed for your baby. You hear people say: "Who asked her to have the child?" or "Was it by force?" A dark place is where you are when God asks you to do something, you are half-way and the storm starts raging. You are battling against storms and rather than move forward, you go round in circles. You are in a dark place when things are so bad and you are fighting dark forces you cannot see.

You find yourself in a difficult place when you are trying to see the light, you become a Christian, give your life to Christ, and then all Hell lets loose. One minute you are on top of the mountain; the next you are in the depth of the valley where it is very dark. Your family is trying to disown you, you have become a pariah, and your parents have even threatened to withdraw funding for your education unless you repent. You have only one choice – degree or deity.

You may have been on your way to the palace and somehow you find yourself in prison. Your secret sin is suddenly found out when the auditors called at work and traced the missing six figures to your account. People now know why you were able to drive those flashy cars and frequently go on exotic holidays. You lose your job, your home and your reputation; and you are now about to lose your freedom – so says the judge.

A dark place is where you are when you visit your local emergency department in the middle of the night for a cough that won't go away, and the next day you are being investigated for cancer. You go to hospital with a nagging headache only for the doctors to find a brain tumour. You have worked hard all your life, got a degree, married the man of your dreams and the next thing you are burying him after he was killed by a drunken truck driver. That must be a very dark place indeed.

A dark place is where you are when your secret flings suddenly come to light; you are about to lose your marriage and you are not sure whether you are going to lose your health too. Your followers desert you, you are confused and heartbroken. You have let yourself and everybody down and you think God is totally mad with you. The only thing you can think of doing is to end it all, and it doesn't matter that your wife, your children and parents are all still alive.

You may already be asking a very relevant question at this point: "These are all dark places, but where is destiny hidden in all these?" I can't blame you for being curious to know. I have asked myself this question many times before and as you read on, you will discover the hidden treasure in dark places. Destiny can surely come out of dark places; you just have to look very closely.

3

Dark Places Are Not New

―――――――

Dark places are not new; the patriarchs had their own share of difficult situations in life. The children of Israel were in slavery in Egypt for 430 years. When Moses the servant of God came to announce to them that God had heard their cries and had decided to set them free and deliver them from their affliction in order to go and worship Him, you can imagine the relief and the joy on their faces. Moses delivered a message from God that Pharaoh should let the people go but he refused. Pharaoh thought the reason they had time to make the request to go and serve God was because they had little or nothing to do with their time. Pharaoh increased their burden and removed straw from their bricks – the Israelites had to look for straw all over the place to mix with mud after the task masters took away their supply.

Rather than things improving, their situation worsened. "Moses, one minute you told us we are getting out of here, the next, our lives have become so miserable," the people cried. Moses found himself in a dark place and the people wanted to stone him. God demonstrated His power and killed all the firstborn of the Egyptians; Pharaoh eventually succumbed and reluctantly let the Israelites go. The children of Israel faced another dark period on their way to the Promised Land – the Red Sea was raging in front and Pharaoh's army was raging behind.

Jacob was in a dark place after he cheated his brother Esau out of his inheritance and he had to run for his dear life. Jacob was exploited by his uncle, Laban, for seven years and he served seven more years to marry Rachel, the woman he really loved. Laban cheated Jacob by changing his wages ten times after he pressured Jacob to stay with him for much longer. Despite serving his father-in-law and uncle for twenty years, Laban vigorously pursued Jacob when he eventually fled. Jacob had to face another dark period in his life not knowing how to appease his brother Esau, who was coming to meet him with a formidable army of three hundred servants. Jacob later wrestled with God until his name was changed to Israel.

Joseph was the son Jacob had in his old age – the apple of his father's eye. Joseph had two big dreams; the next minute he was thrown into perpetual darkness and his dreams turned into nightmares. His brothers, who were intimidated by his dreams, abandoned their initial plan to kill him, and dumped him in a pit instead. They later sold Joseph to the Ishmaelites and he was taken to Egypt as a slave. Potiphar's wife falsely accused Joseph of attempted rape when he refused to sleep with her due to his fear of God and he ended up in jail. He was forgotten by someone he helped in prison but he kept the dream in his heart. Joseph was a man in bondage for 13 years – he went from his father's house to the pit and from the pit to prison. It became darker and darker for him.

Gideon found himself in a very dark situation after the Israelites were ravaged by the Midianites. The angel of the Lord appeared to him and said: "The Lord is with you, you mighty man of valour!" (Judges 6:12). Gideon then said to the angel: "O my lord, if the LORD is with us, why then has all this happened to us? And where are all His miracles which our fathers told us about? Did not the LORD bring us up from Egypt? But now the LORD has forsaken us and delivered us into the hands of the Midianites." (Judges 6:13). Gideon asked the angel for a sign after he was told he would be the one to deliver Israel from their enemies. To reassure him, God touched his first offering with fire and asked him to make a second offering with the items which his people used to worship false gods. Still not sure and afraid, Gideon cut wood from the Asherah pole and offered a second bull offering in the night because he was afraid of his family and the townspeople.

Elimelech relocated to the country of Moab due to famine in Judah and took his wife Naomi and his two sons Mahlon and Chilion with him. Elimelech later died and his two sons married Moabite women – Ruth and Orpah. Ruth found herself in a dark place when her husband and her brother-in-law died in the land of the Moabites. Naomi, her mother-in-law, decided to head back to her homeland. Ruth did not have any child to validate her place in the family, and Naomi asked her to go back to her own people. Your situation may not be that you don't have a child; it might be that you have no status, no school certificate, or university degree to secure your place where you think you belong. And it can be dark to feel rejected and unwanted. Orpah returned to her family but Ruth clung to Naomi and did not waver.

Again you are asking: "Where is destiny in all this?"

The story of Jabez exemplified a dark period in the life of a man who was going nowhere. Everybody likes to hear the sound of their name but not Jabez. He was given the name "sorrow" or "the one that causes sorrow" which he carried with him everywhere he went. It was like disaster struck wherever you found Jabez and he lived with this burden until he called upon the God of Heaven.

Samson also found himself in a dark place when, rather than save his people, he abandoned his God-given assignment and formed an alliance with his enemies. He was thrown into perpetual darkness when his eyes were plucked out after the woman he loved betrayed him into the hands of the Philistines. Samson, a man called to save his people, later cried to God to die with his enemies – it was a very dark situation for him.

David experienced more dark periods than most people – what appears to be an undesirable conception was followed by an unwelcomed and uncelebrated birth. David was banished to the desert outback to look after the sheep while his seven brothers lounged at home. David's friends were dumb sheep and his enemies were lions and bears. His father had totally forgotten about him when Samuel visited Jesse's house to anoint one of his sons as king. When David's breakthrough finally came, he faced Goliath who had defied the Israelite army for forty days. You might be forgiven for thinking that defeating Goliath would be the end of all David's problems, but he had to run away from Saul who became jealous of his new celebrity status, and he moved from cave to cave running for his dear life.

Even ascending the throne and winning battles did not spare David from staring death in the face. His own people wanted to stone him after the Amalekites took away his wives and children, and everything belonging to his men. David found himself in another dark period of his life when instead of going to battle when all kings went to war, he stayed back at home. He then saw Bathsheba bathing naked and committed adultery with his army general's wife. He became a murderer after he engineered the killing of Uriah in battle and took Bathsheba to be one of his wives. David's sin was exposed when God placed His righteous finger upon his life; he was broken-hearted when Nathan the prophet confronted him, and more so when the child from that sexual liaison with Bathsheba was not spared by God.

You may wonder "How can anything good come out of all this?" Please stay with me.

You may have heard the call of God on your life, or God may have asked you to do something great, and then, all Hell let loose, and opposition arose. Sometimes while you are trying to do the will of God, people who should be helping you try so hard to get you in trouble. Your situation is not different from that of Nehemiah who answered the call of God to go and rebuild the wall of the city of Jerusalem. On Nehemiah's return, he was opposed by Sanballat the Horonite, Tobiah the Ammonite and Geshem the Arab – they tried to discourage Nehemiah, and they mocked, ridiculed and opposed him. When they could not stop Nehemiah and his men, they tried to distract him by asking him to come down for a dialogue. They sent letters to Nehemiah, not once, but four times. When this did not work, Sanballat sent an aide to Nehemiah with an open letter in which he spread rumours and made false accusations that Nehemiah and the Jews were plotting to revolt against the king.

Have you ever felt that your detractors will go to any lengths and even use the name of God to put you into darkness? Does anybody want you dead because you have chosen to do the will of God? Nehemiah was in the same position. Sanballat and Tobiah were crafty men; after Sanballat's attempts to intimidate Nehemiah did not work, he devised another plot – he hired Shemiah the son of Deliah to persuade Nehemiah to meet them in the temple – the house of God. You may ask: "What could be wrong with a godly man going to the house of God to meet someone?" The problem was that Nehemiah's detractors wanted to lure him there to kill him. Nehemiah realised God had not sent Shemiah and that Shemiah was hired by his enemies. Nehemiah replied: "I will not go down".

You may find yourself in a dark place even after you have done great exploits for God. Elijah killed the false prophets of Baal and then Jezebel later threatened his life. Elijah dropped from a great heroic moment of victory to a miserable moment of despair when a woman said he only had 24 hours to live. Elijah ran helter-skelter, despaired of life, and asked God to kill him. God, however, had another assignment for him and dispatched him off to Syria. God reassured Elijah that he had another seven thousand men who had not bowed their knees to Baal. You must know that even while you are in darkness, God has greater plans for you.

You may not be recognised for what you are or what you do, or you may have been betrayed by others. Jesus was "on the shelf" for about thirty years of His life even though He had a great mission to accomplish. He was betrayed to death for thirty pieces of silver by one of His disciples. He was disappointed by the disciples whom He asked to pray with Him for one hour. He was deserted by those He loved and denied by Peter when it mattered most. He was rejected by His people who pleaded for murderers and thieves to be released in His place. While on the cross, His accusers despised Him, spat on Him, and shared His clothing. When Jesus was in excruciating pain, He turned to God to spare Him the agony but the Father turned His face away from the Son.

God did not spare His own Son from the death of the cross. Jesus Christ, the creator of the ends of the Earth was unceremoniously hung on the cross after His tormentors beat Him, spat on Him and ridiculed Him. He died at the hands of the people He came to save – nothing in life could be darker than that. Darkness fell upon the Earth and the veil that separated man from God was torn forever. Jesus was laid in a borrowed tomb, and soldiers guarded His dead body. He found Himself in Hell where He contended with principalities and powers that wanted to hold Him bound. Pandemonium broke out in Hell and the powers of darkness rejoiced. At last, they had got their man; the demons rejoiced – the Saviour of mankind had finally been delivered into their hands.

I will never forget this proverb: "When death takes away your defence, it is sending you a strong signal." Nothing could be truer than in the case of Jesus' disciples who were thrown into the dark when their Master, Teacher, and Lord was taken away from them. They lost their support, their spiritual compass and their defence. The reality of their new life hit them; they became disillusioned and many returned to their old ways. That is what darkness does to you – you return to what you had left behind.

What about those who came after Jesus? They all faced dark situations at one point or another. Peter, Stephen, the other disciples and Apostle Paul; John Wesley, Finis Dake, Martin Luther King (Junior), Kenneth Hagin, Billy Graham, David Oyedepo, Joyce Meyer and the T.D. Jakes of this world – they all had to carry their crosses. Darkness spares no one.

4

Darkness Spares No One

All of us have experienced being in dark places in our lives, whether it is caused by Satan or others, situations or circumstances, disobedience or foolishness. I may have described your dark place, and I may not have referred to yours at all. It does not matter; we all go through dark places at one point or another. Yours may not be like mine and mine may not have the same impact as yours, but they are equally important. The darkest periods in my life are nothing compared to that of many others you will read in this book, but you will learn one or two things from my story.

Only a few people can boast of having four mothers as I had when I was growing up. I call these people "mother" because unless someone told you or you were very close to my family, you wouldn't know the difference. My first mother was my younger aunt, my second was my step-mother, the third was my biological mother and my fourth mother was my older aunt. All of them except for my biological mother Mary have since departed to be with the Lord.

I was born into a polygamous family and as far as I was aware my mother was the second woman in my father's life. They were not married even according to the Yoruba tradition in south-west Nigeria in the sixties. My father had always been a very good man, but he could not resist the love of many women who wanted to bear his name. For some strange reason, possibly rooted in tribal differences between the places where my parents came from, my biological mother's family did not want her married to my father. My mother returned to her hometown when I was only two years old under the pretext of going to look after her sick mother. She never returned and I was left in the care of my father and his extended family.

My father's younger sister took over as my mother for a while and then passed me on to my step-mother. I grew up to know my father's first wife as my "real" mother. Abbey, my step-mother's first son, was only two days older than me. We were "twin brothers" except that we were from different mothers. My father, as you may have guessed, was playing "home and away" at the time. Amazingly, two women had two boys for him forty-eight hours apart, one on New Year's Eve, the other a day after the New Year. My father would have received many congratulations at the time and probably was envied by many of his mates. That would be seen as a sign of male virility in those days, and something to brag about.

I did not suffer any abuse or neglect at the hand of my step-mother. I did not even know the difference at the time. I ate the same food as the other children and put on the same clothes as my "twin brother" Abbey. While growing up, I went to places I later realised were my step-mother's extended family home, and I commanded other children as if I belonged there. I could not remember anyone saying to me at anytime "You don't belong here". If you are from the African culture you may understand better the significance of this. If you don't belong to a traditional extended family house (either by reason of birth or marriage), with all I did, someone should have asked me to my face, "Whose son are you?" or "Who do you think you are?" Strangely nobody did!

Even now, and having thought hard about it, I wouldn't have wanted anything different regarding the way I was brought up or treated by my step-mother. As far as my father was concerned, once you were fed, clothed, and sent to school, there was nothing to complain or worry about. My step-mother (I mean my second mother) was a great woman, who instilled discipline and hard work, and she was industrious too – she could sell ice blocks at the North Pole or sand in the Sahara Desert. I would stay in her shop and sell Coca-Cola, and sometimes take it to the local bus garage to sell when the drinks were not moving quickly enough. With the ever blazing African sun and the temperature in the thirties, you could be sure of making a quick sale at the garage. I was my mother's 'accountant' and 'treasurer' and we were very close. She was the type of woman that would brood over you like a hen over her chickens, particularly when I had done something wrong and my father was ready to use the cane.

I grew up with my father and step-mother until the age of 11. One day, as if my step-mother knew what was going to happen, she called me aside and said, "I want to tell you something but I don't know how to say it." And then there was a silence that seemed to last forever. My step-mother summoned up courage and said, "I am not your real mother you know; when you next have your school summer holiday, ask your father to take you to your own mother." She really tried her best to make it sound simple and nice. At first I thought she was trying to wind me up, but when she repeated it again, I began to think she was very serious. There was a thick silence in the room – you could cut it with a knife. My mother was frozen too, tears welling up in her eyes. I managed to hold back my tears, I couldn't believe what I had just heard.

For a while I thought I was dreaming but I knew I was standing facing my mother, and not in bed. I even thought that my mother was playing a trick but it was no "April fool" – we were in June and approaching the end of the third term at school. Being my mother's greatest confidant, I knew when my mother was serious about something. That was for real! Even now that I write about it, I can still picture her face and remember clearly how a cold chill ran down my spine the moment I was given that bombshell.

As a young 11-year-old boy, all the security of a caring mother and family that I had held on to so dearly fell apart in an instant.

My life was thrown into a sort of darkness; my composure turned into anger. How could my mother do such a thing? Why would she want me to see her as my step-mother, and my "twin-brother", Abbey, as my step-brother? *"We are not step-brothers; we are twins and that's the way we'll be forever,"* I thought to myself. I tried to reverse the situation, but I had no power at all. All these years, I had had the security of a loving mother and a caring family; now everything had been blown apart. I was confused, angry and hurt. I wanted to be like some of the other kids – with one father and one mother. I now had two mothers – one I knew, the other I knew not. It would have been easier to move on or to discard my step-mother only if I had been treated badly, but she was not that type. You couldn't have asked for a better mother in life.

Mary, my biological mother, became the third mother I had in my very short life. Even though I met Mary shortly afterwards, the bond was not really there initially and it took many years for that to happen. After the school holiday, I returned to live with my father and my step-mother (I mean my second mother). I said to myself that I knew that I had to live with the reality of having two mothers but my step-mother was my real mother – I tried to convince myself. For a long time I suffered from identity crisis and wondered why I had to be in that particular position, and why my biological mother would not just come back. I had no one to ask these pertinent questions; I asked myself many times but got no answer.

I can imagine someone reading this saying, "How on earth could that be counted as a dark period in your life? After all, you have a father and a mother, and two mothers even. An orphan has neither. How can that be a dark period for you?" The truth is: that was a very dark period indeed if you look at it with the eyes of a child. Fear, feelings of rejection and abandonment, identity crisis, hopelessness, frustration and anger were part of the package. My situation was equally as dark as that of millions of children all over the world caught up in situations they know nothing about, and for many who are trapped in situations of wars, natural disasters, hunger, poverty, sickness, disease, and in hospitals, mental homes and orphanages.

It became even darker

18 January 1981 is a day I will never forget. As if my situation was not dark enough, my step-mother (my second mother) died suddenly, possibly of hypertension and stress. The news of her death came as a very rude shock to my system and to everyone who knew her; it was made even more difficult to comprehend as I never knew her to be sick or suffering from any medical condition. Remember the proverb I wrote about before: "When death takes away your defence, it is sending you a strong signal." My defence was gone forever. It became even darker!

My father

My father was, and still is, a very nice man but he was never good at saying "no" to the women who wanted to bear his name. He even adopted other people's children as his own. My father is the type that if he saw a mother or a father struggling to cope in bringing up their children on their own, he would say something like this: "Don't worry, the boy can stay with me and when things get better, you can come and take him." When the mother or the father came back to take their child, my father would say: "Your boy is a good lad, he's got used to this place. Why don't you leave him here with his brothers and sisters? I will send him back when he has finished his secondary school education." That was it – many of my father's "adopted children" never left his house until after their university or college education. I could count at least three of them who never left my father's house until they got married. That was the kind of person he was, and he does the same even now.

As the children grew up in age and in numbers, the family

house became busier and noisier. Polygamy took its toll; whatever love, affection and resources my father had were shared among his ten children and a few others he 'adopted'. It became more difficult to read, concentrate, focus on my studies or plan for the future while living in my father's house. The darkest place a man can be in life is to have great potential and never realise it. I knew I had to do something quickly if I didn't want to end up living a life of lack in the middle of plenty. Education was my gateway out of poverty and I decided to take my studies very seriously.

Studying in the dark

Studying at that time was not easy – the nearest functioning library was about seven miles away in the middle of Dugbe, a large noisy market in Ibadan (the largest city in the southwest of Nigeria). As an alternative, I regularly sneaked into a dilapidated primary school classroom near a very busy football stadium (Liberty) at weekends. I usually clambered in through one of the windows to avoid being spotted by the security guards. The guards in those days were usually elderly men, widely feared, rightly or wrongly for their acclaimed *juju* (black magic or voodoo) power to catch intruders, burglars or armed robbers. Some of them had locally made rifles (*shakabulas*) which might or might not be working. I was very careful about my mission; I chose the classroom whose window was farthest away from the main road. Once inside, the holes in the rusty classroom's corrugated iron roofing sheets provided me with the much-needed light to read without opening any of the windows.

I studied in the dark and started scoring top marks in my school work and gained respect from my peers and teachers. Everything was going well with my study at weekends until one day when I heard a hard knock on the door – it was the security man! The elderly man in his sixties shouted: "Who are you? I know you are in there, come out. Who are you?" I kept quiet; my heart was beating fast. I tried to recite Psalm 23 – "The Lord Is My

Shepherd" but I could not remember any word or phrase past the second line – "I shall not want". I could hear the man's footsteps pacing outside the door in the school compound and knew he was getting desperate. The elderly man shouted again: "Who are you? I know you are in there, come out now or I will curse you."

Curse me for what? *"For reading my books?"* – I asked myself. No one would wait for the curse of an elderly man reputed to have *juju* power. I had to act fast, and I had only two options – either I jump out through the window on the other side and be caught as a burglar, or I open the door from the inside, surrender to the elderly man and explain my mission. I didn't know what was awaiting me outside the classroom on either side, and I didn't have all the time in the world to decide. I opted for the latter, and opened the door. If the guard was waiting to catch a serial burglar or a notorious armed robber, he was mistaken. I was caught with a bag full of my own books.

Unknown to me, people who lived nearby had probably seen me climb through the window over a period of time and had informed the guard. The guard normally would be afraid of losing his job if anything was stolen from the school, but I can't imagine anything of value that was worth stealing in that classroom. I told the guard I was very sorry for being a nuisance and explained that I had only sneaked into the classroom because I had nowhere quiet to read. I could see the relief on his face – his job was secure.

To my surprise, the elderly man burst into tears, and said: "You are a very small boy; and you are breaking into a classroom just to read your book; if only my own [children] could be like you; I have to beg my children to do their school work not to talk of studying." The man then offered me a "free pass" to come and study in the school any time I wanted – on the condition that I reported to him first. I took up the offer for a while and studied very hard with good results. After a while, another older guard replaced the elderly gentleman that gave me the free pass. I knew my time was up; I had to move on. I never wanted to relive another encounter with a second guard with *juju*. It was at that point, at the age of 15, when I moved to live with my father's older sister (my fourth mother).

Staying with my aunt helped me to focus better and she being a strict disciplinarian and a Christian set me on a good path. I also found a role model in my cousin, Sam, to whom I will forever be grateful. I will tell you more about him in Chapter 8. I was taught how to make different dishes but sometimes the children had to wake up at five in the morning when my aunt fancied eating her favourite 'Akara' (fried bean balls). You first soak the beans early in the morning, peel off the skin one or two hours later, and then manually grind the beans on a stone until they form a smooth paste. This is what blenders do nowadays but I can tell you the taste is not the same – particularly when the 'Akara' was eaten with fresh hot bread just coming out of the oven from the bakery next door. Once the bean balls are fried, you allow them to cool down while the family embark on an hour-long prayer session. Those prayers helped shape the next decades of my life.

5

A Study In Darkness

I could fill this book with stories about dark places, but this is not my aim. I want to explore in greater detail what dark places are, and what a merciful God can do with dark periods in peoples' lives. I don't profess to be an expert on this subject but I have learned a few things over the years. A proper understanding of these characteristics will help you to look in the right places on your way out of a difficult situation.

Dark places are very dark; they are places where you cannot see much or where you cannot see at all. They are places where you are likely to fall or to stumble, places where the irrational becomes rational. A dark place is where you are likely to lose your reputation and start to offend people – you start to blame your spouse or your mother-in-law, your teacher or the school's principal, your boyfriend or his mother, your ex-spouse or her sister, your boss or your manager, your pastor or even God.

The darkest places in the universe are very cold. The same is true when people are going through dark periods in their lives. You may feel people are cold and don't give a damn. Sometimes people don't! People may withdraw their warmth and affection, reject or snub you. Sometimes people aren't cold, yet you perceive coldness and relate negatively to others because of that. People who are trying to be nice don't even know what to say or do in order not to offend you. Others who say they understand your situation don't, even when they think they are very close to you. One astronaut who had just returned from a Shuttle mission said, "I didn't know what black was until I'd been in space." God is the only one that understands every situation and the one who has the true solution.

If you ask a million people where the darkest place on Earth is, you'll probably get a million answers. Some have said it is Lake Vostok, Antarctica, which is around 230 kilometres long and 50 kilometres wide. The lake has a maximum water depth of over 500 metres. The permanently cold (up to –88°C), dark, pressurised environment of Lake Vostok is considered to pose serious challenges to survival, and could result in the discovery of novel organisms and processes. That looks like a very dark place to me. In life's dark situations, survival might be threatened and people could turn out to be what they never imagined to be, and do strange and ridiculous things.

A dark place is likely to be dim, dingy and dangerous; a place where creepy creatures lie. It is a place where you are likely to fall, trip on people or slip up; a place where you are vulnerable and where people think little of you. It is a place where rather than help you, people plot your downfall. You are going through a divorce and your spouse is trying to take your house and children away; and your lawyers are ready to milk you dry. You are weak and people are trying to take advantage of you. You are being asked to borrow more money to pay off your debt and sink deeper into a financial abyss. You are being offered ridiculous amounts to sell your business, properties or house. You are being asked to take a pay cut or leave your job, fit in or get out, serve God or serve the devil. You can't sit on the fence, every which way you are stuck and don't know what to do.

People have a tendency to throw things in dark places; while life has thrown its full blow at you, people are also throwing their rubbish in your face. And to make it worse, they think they are doing you a favour or giving you advice. You may find yourself in a dark place because you are not married or have no life partner. You may have been single, divorced, separated or widowed for a long time. Initially people are mindful of what to say but now they say to your face: "You are getting too old, you'd better settle down with him; he's the only thing you've got; you won't be the first one to end up with a married man."

A familiar environment becomes strange when people go through difficulties – they may start to feel they are not welcome in places they have been accustomed to. You may find yourself in an unfamiliar place when the house which used to be your home becomes a place you have to write to or call ahead of time before you can visit. You are in an unfamiliar place when after you separate from your partner or are divorced, you now have to visit other people's houses or attend a visiting centre to see your children. Your children have now become strangers and want to run away from you. Life becomes unfamiliar when you are sacked from work and given only a few minutes to pack your belongings. An unfamiliar place is where you are when you have to apply for a job at a company that previously belonged to you. The prodigal son was in such an unfamiliar place when he had to return to his father's house to beg for one of the servants' jobs.

A dark place can be very stuffy; a place where it is difficult to breathe and where you feel everything is being thrown at you. Problems in dark places don't come one at a time – as if one is not enough, another hits you while you are trying to grapple with the first. People may go around making up what they don't know about you, your circumstances or situation. Others who think they have an idea may even appoint themselves as experts in your life. And God help you if you don't take their advice.

Nobody wants to go to a dark place. It is a place where everything is silent or scary; full of strange and horrible noises, a place where rational becomes irrational and a place where the familiar becomes unfamiliar. It is a place where you find you cannot trust anyone; you become very careful or too careful and sometimes miss the very person God has sent to help you. A dark place is a place of emptiness where you are depressed, where you want to cry but can't find tears. It is a place of loneliness; a place where "it is so near but yet so far". You feel like giving up, because you think there is no hope for the future.

All is not dark even in the dark

It can be so dark that sometimes we fail to realise that good things can come out of adversity. Cavett Robert, the famous writer once said: "If we study the lives of great men and women carefully and unemotionally we find that, invariably, greatness was developed, tested and revealed through the darker periods of their lives. One of the largest tributaries of the river of greatness is always the stream of adversity." Writer Napoleon Hill also said, "Every adversity carries with it the seed of an equivalent or greater benefit."

None of us like dark periods in our lives but destiny can be hidden in dark places. Dark periods can be places to mark the end of one chapter in life and begin another. I listened to Bishop Mark Chirona in July 2010 when he spoke about going through one door to another. As you move forward in life, you close one door while you enter another. It was easy for me to relate to what Bishop Chirona said as I have worked in secure units with air locks for over a decade. Imagine yourself going through a set of two doors in which you have to close one before you can open the other; at some point you will find yourself in a pathway or passage where nothing happens – often quiet, lonely and empty. The space has little or no room for excess baggage; and you are selective about what you take with you. Without passing through that quiet, lonely, empty and sometimes dark pathway you will not get to the other door that leads to a new chapter in your life. The pathway is what we fear most, but it is not the destination.

Some of us do not take stock until we find ourselves in a big mess. A dark place can be a place of rest, a place to refresh and a place to take stock. It is a place to listen to what God has to say for your life; a place to gain strength, build character, and a place to strategise for the future. Dark places may afford you the right opportunity to think clearly on what has happened and where you are currently, to change perspectives and to think about what to do next. Lack of perspective is what makes people run helter-skelter, from pillar to post, hurting others and pulling people down along a destructive path.

Someone in the dark might think their husband or wife, friend or boss, or their daughter's boyfriend or mother-in-law is their problem, and focus on how to get back at them or how to get through to them. Others may be responsible in some cases, but the real problem is the devil. I am not suggesting in any way that the devil is responsible for everything, but ultimately anything that does not originate from God can only be of the devil or his devices. When the storm began in Matthew 8:24, the boat carrying Jesus and the disciples was filling up with water. Jesus did not rebuke the water; he rebuked the wind. Something is behind the storm and that is what you need to deal with. It takes God's grace and the right perspective to identify the real problem and then deal with it.

6

When You Are In A Hole

No one wants to be in darkness, especially when they can afford not to be. When you find yourself in a situation that looks dark and hopeless, the urge to do something or anything can be very tempting. It is a normal and natural reaction to want to act when something is bothering you or when something bad has just happened – you move swiftly when your status or well-being is threatened. Some have described this as "self-preservation". What most people do is to go into automatic pilot of a sort, or a reflex reaction to deal with a perceived danger, an excruciating pain or unseen spiritual forces.

In your attempts to fix a bad situation you may act hurriedly or not act at all, make bad decisions or act in a negative or destructive manner. The devil does not care what you do as long as you are not acting according to the will of God. The devil wants to add salt to your injury and you must be aware of his devices. The number one rule when you find yourself in a hole is not to dig further. If you find yourself in a dark situation, don't do just anything or engage in self-pity, blame yourself or blame others. Don't go out to seek revenge or make up your mind that you will never forgive or forget. It is very easy to become bitter, to give up, and to act out when you find yourself in a dark place. You must avoid this at all costs.

Do nothing!

Do nothing! Do I really mean that? Yes, I do, and it might surprise you. This is one of the most important and most difficult things to do when you find yourself in a difficult situation. The temptation to do something or to be seen to be doing something is always there and can be huge. Do nothing – look before you leap and think before you act. It is important to hear clearly from God and not to dig yourself into more trouble. If you're already in a hole don't dig further. Don't dig into more pain, don't hurt more people, don't accuse more people, don't borrow more money, don't cause more offences, don't cause more distress and certainly, don't plot more revenge. Be still and know that He is God; let Him fight the battle for you.

You are more likely to be wrong when you do something just for the sake of it or act under pressure because of what people say or think. You will act in error most times if you make a decision when you are distressed. When I worked for a lady several years ago, I informed my boss about a particular junior doctor who had been disrespectful and rude to me, and asked for her advice. My boss said to me: "John, I know you want an answer right now; but go home tonight and sleep over it; if by tomorrow morning you still feel strongly about what you want to do the same way you feel right now, then consider doing it." Thank God for wise women (and men); not making a rushed decision is one approach that has served me well for many years and I have used it on several occasions to help others. I did not invent it; I learnt it from others, and it works.

Avoid isolation

Don't isolate yourself when you are in the dark – nobody would notice you were there! It is okay for you to have a quiet time alone to reflect, but don't avoid people. God put the solitary in families; only a lonely person suffers alone. I have met a few people who when going through difficult times become insular – they cut themselves off from everyone, stop going out, delete numbers from their phones or cut their phones off altogether. Their demeanour screams from afar: "Don't you ever come near me!" The problem is: others may be going through their own wilderness and may not even notice you are suffering. At one point in my life I wanted to disconnect God TV, a Christian channel which had helped my faith and sharpened my cutting edge over the years. As I picked up the phone to cancel the subscription, God said to me: *"That's exactly what the devil is waiting for."*

It is not possible to open up to everyone that comes your way but you must find the God-ordained connections in your life in difficult times. Don't become insular and shut yourself off from help or good advice. An isolated person is easy prey for the devil and God never intended for anyone to be without encouragement, support and care. Connect yourself with those that will lift you up when you are down and weak. Go to church, attend home fellowships, join prayer meetings, and visit other well-meaning people. Don't forgo your social outlets – a day out with the girls (or boys), family meets, friends' reunion, dinner parties, get-togethers and the like – they are all equally important.

Don't indulge in self-pity

Self-pity can be comforting initially; it does not last long and then it becomes a burden. Self-pity has a tendency to temporarily anaesthetise your pain, but paralyses your thoughts, feelings and actions – you must resist it. Don't call a "pity party" even when you think people might find it strange that you are not wearing a sad sorry face. A person who indulges in self-pity cannot and will not accept the reality of their situation or responsibility for their own life. The tendency is then to blame someone else; which brings me to my next point.

People who wallow in self-pity go around in a bad mood, feeling sorry for themselves. They think that they are in a bad situation because of someone else, which occasionally may be true, but many times it is not. The easiest thing to do when something bad happens is to blame your spouse, your friend, parents, teacher, employer, college, pastor or God. Stuff happens, and sometimes there is no one to blame. Blaming others is childish – children blame others as they have not learnt to be responsible for their actions. The blame game makes it difficult for you to change and keeps you in a weak position; you adopt the victim role and ascribe to others too much power that no man should ever be given.

Worry

Avoid worrying; it adds nothing to your life but takes joy, peace and sleep from you. The Bible says in Matthew 6:25–32:

> Therefore I say to you, do not worry about your life, what you will eat or what you will drink; nor about your body, what you will put on. Is not life more than food and the body more than clothing? Look at the birds of the air, for they neither sow nor reap nor gather into barns; yet your heavenly Father feeds them. Are you not of more value than they? Which of you by worrying can add one cubit to his stature? So why do you worry about clothing? Consider the lilies of the field, how they grow: they neither toil nor spin; and yet I say to you that even Solomon in all his glory was not arrayed like one of these. Now if God so clothes the grass of the field, which today is, and tomorrow is thrown into the oven, *will He* not much more *clothe* you, O you of little faith? Therefore do not worry, saying, "What shall we eat?" or "What shall we drink?" or "What shall we wear?" For after all these things the Gentiles seek. For your heavenly Father knows that you need all these things.

The devil can use worry as a stronghold. I will never forget when I worked as a junior psychiatrist in the nineties. One of my patients was a lady in her fifties who had been admitted to different hospitals on and off for 20 years – she suffered from severe depression and anxiety. She had become extremely worrisome about her life and future after her husband left her for her best friend, six years after they got married. That was a terrible thing to happen to anyone and I will not in any way attempt to minimise her sufferings. Her worries turned into mild and moderate depression, and then into severe treatment-resistant depression. The enemy used her situation as a stronghold in her life. She remained the same despite using old and new antidepressants, psychology and electric shock treatments (Electro-convulsive therapy, ECT). I knew at that point that her recovery was not in the hands of doctors or psychologists – she needed God. Unfortunately, we were not allowed to preach the word of God to patients. Five years later she died in that hospital – she slept one day and never woke up! Sadly, she wasn't the last person I knew that suffered a similar fate.

Bitterness and unforgiveness

In 1996, I was sacked from one of my jobs in Lagos, Nigeria after highlighting health and safety concerns at the hospital where I worked. I secured another job shortly afterwards but I wanted to avenge my hurt and humiliation, more so as I had bills to pay and a young family to feed. I plotted daily how to expose the problems to the medical regulatory bodies. I wanted the hospital to lose business from their individual patients and company contracts. I spoke to anyone that cared to listen about the evil being perpetrated by my former employer. I was bitter, and it didn't take my new employer long to notice. My new boss called me one day and said: "I know you are angry about the way you were treated. Don't use all your energy to pursue negative things when there are many positive things you can focus your life on." Something clicked and the light came on. My boss was not even a born-again Christian at the time. I have used that phrase many times in the last few years and sometimes I forget that I did not coin it originally.

Hurt people who are bitter have tendencies to hurt others. I once heard Dr Creflo Dollar put it this way: "Hurt people hurt people". I remember the story of a lady who was jilted by her fiancé a few months after their engagement. She was very bitter and felt humiliated and ashamed. She vowed she would break as many hearts as possible to avenge her hurt. True to her words, she embarked on a heart-breaking mission and left several men as casualties on her destructive path. Over a four-year period, she lured men into very intimate relationships, raised their hopes about them living "happily ever after" and dropped them flat when they were most vulnerable. She inflicted severe hurt on several would-be grooms, their friends and their families. Her escapade gave her a sense of power and she thought she had had the last laugh. One day, she decided she had had enough and wanted to settle down. By that time she had contracted AIDS (HIV infection) and only had herself to blame.

The devil wants you to become bitter when you find yourself in a dark place. That is the quickest way to miss out on your destiny. Two wrongs can never make a right. Put simply, you cannot right a wrong with another wrong. Worry and unforgiveness are the essential ingredients of bitterness – they grow bigger as you focus on the problem. You must not seek revenge or the downfall of your afflictors – leave everything to God. He is the great avenger and the one that fights for someone without a deliverer. Don't follow after those who leave the way of uprightness to walk in the way of darkness (Proverbs 2:13). Focus your attention on God.

Acting out

Some people are prone to acting out when they find themselves in trouble. This can be in the form of revenge as exemplified by the story of the lady who contracted AIDS in her attempt to seek revenge. Acting out could also be in the form of domestic violence or seeking illegitimate reliefs, abuse of alcohol and illegal drugs, pornography, gambling, illicit sexual liaisons and adultery. Other behaviour such as over-eating, excessive spending beyond one's means and excessive working to earn more money in order to prove a point are equally damaging.

Don't give up

In my career as a psychiatrist, I have seen many people whom the devil managed to persuade to give up on their dreams. The devil negotiated them out of their destiny by persuading them that their pain was unbearable, that no one cared, that God had forgotten them and that they could never make it. Nothing could be further from the truth; and the society we live in does not help matters. These people end their own lives, leaving families and children to a life of pain, hurt and misery. The tragic irony is that the life taken doesn't even belong to them – it belongs to God.

A man came to me several years ago after experiencing significant challenges in his marriage. He felt his wife and children did not appreciate him despite all he had done for them. What was most painful for him was his perception that he was being taken for granted. He said to me: "She thinks I'm stupid". The man also felt humiliated when his wife threatened to call the police to arrest him, something that is not uncommon among quarrelling couples living in the West, including many living in diaspora.

I counselled the man for an hour and I thought I had done a very good job. When he was about to leave he heaved a heavy sigh and said, "I can't cope with this any longer ... I'll just go home, kill her, kill the children and kill myself." With the look in his eyes, he was serious! Even my experience as a psychiatrist did not prepare me for that. It would have been easier if he was one of my patients; but he was not. He was someone I had known socially, not in a professional capacity. I remember saying to the distressed gentleman, "You are the only one who knows a hundred per cent that you are not stupid". I am sure I told him other silly things which I cannot remember now. I was ready to call the police if he had not changed his mind. Eventually the man calmed down and decided not to embark on a killing spree. I am not sure what worked that day but I knew God stepped into the situation; otherwise you would have been reading a different account today.

Giving up may not be as serious as the case of the gentleman described above; it might be as simple as packing up, leaving your family and your loved ones to go and live abroad, divorcing your spouse, running off with another man or woman, leaving your work or even your local church. Sometimes when people give up, they think the pasture is greener on the other side. I must warn you it is not always the case.

The story of Naomi and her husband Elimelech in the book of Ruth (Chapter 1) provides a salutary lesson which is often overlooked. When there was famine in Bethlehem, Judah, Elimelech, his wife Naomi and their two sons, Mahlon and Chilion emigrated to live in the country of Moab. No one could blame Elimelech for wanting to provide for his family – that is what any sensible and respectable man will do. The problem however was that Moab was a place full of sexual immorality and worship of idols. Going to Moab is like meeting a legitimate need with an illegitimate resource. People, unsurprisingly, do unthinkable things when they find themselves in darkness.

Elimelech's sons formed an alliance with the enemies of God and married their daughters. Within a short space of time, Elimelech and his two sons died. Naomi became a widow and her two daughters-in-law lost their husbands. That was tragic indeed! Naomi had no choice than to go back to the land she ran away from. The pasture had not been as green as expected. She told her daughters-in-law to go back to their Moabite families but Ruth refused, and cleaved unto her. When Naomi eventually returned to Bethlehem, the entire city was excited because of them. Why? The women of the city must have heard about the tragedy that had befallen Naomi and her family. I am sure they probably thought she was dead, and they said: "Is this Naomi?"

Yes, it was Naomi. Notice that despite the famine, the people of the city were still there; they even recognised Naomi when she returned. The famine which Elimelech and his family ran away from had not killed off the people. Famine represents lack and you can find yourself in a dark place because you lack certain things in your life – fulfilment, joy, money, status, a job, a life partner or a child. Important as these needs are, they are not reasons to become desperate. Some people will go as far as committing atrocities and crimes or consulting the occult to meet needs in their life. Be warned – it can only end in tears.

You must be careful what you do when life throws its challenges at you. Don't put yourself in an environment where you are dining with the enemy and where you are taken away from the service and worship of your God, or from the love and support of your family. God is the true solution in your life; you must put your focus on Him. There are many things you can do in dark places. You can shine the light of God in darkness and you will learn about these in the next chapter.

7

Lighting Up In The Dark

When you find yourself in a difficult situation, many questions will be going through your mind and you may ask yourself, "What do I do now?" I will explore in this chapter how to react when the enemy threatens you and when you find yourself in a dark place. These suggestions are by no means exhaustive but I believe you will find one or two things useful as you read on. Here are some of the things you must do if you want to achieve a good outcome.

Be quiet

Quietness is one of the spiritual disciplines that I have learnt to practise over the years, and it works. It is only when you are quiet and still in your mind and spirit that you can clearly hear what God is saying. When I am troubled over a difficulty or a challenge, I go somewhere quiet to think and to hear from God. It may be in my study or in the garden, but it's usually in my bedroom. When you hear what God is saying you will receive direction and know what to do next. The reason why many people cannot be still and be quiet is that they don't know God; and when faced with challenges, would rather run up and down, looking for help where there is none. I don't know about you, but I have been in that position many times in the past when I burnt away my physical, emotional and even spiritual energy trying to fix what should be left in God's hand. "Be still, and know that I am God" (Psalm 46:10) – that's the word of the Lord.

You must humble yourself in your quietness, confess your misdeeds and repent of your sins in order to move on. The Bible says:

> If My people who are called by My name will humble themselves, and pray and seek My face, and turn from their wicked ways, then I will hear from heaven, and will forgive their sin and heal their land. (2 Chronicles 7:14)

Humbling yourself is not the same thing as going on a guilt trip or calling a pity party. It is important to acknowledge what has happened, the part you have played or have not played in the matter, and then move on. You may ask: "Is it that easy to move on?" Yes, move on or forever stay where you are. The shackles have already been broken; you wouldn't be here if the problem was greater than you. It's your responsibility and no one else's to move on.

Be real to yourself

Be true to yourself when you're going through a dark period of life. There is nothing new under the sun and there is no new affliction anywhere that hasn't happened to someone before. It's liberating to acknowledge one's situation – if you find yourself in difficulty or darkness, acknowledge it. Acknowledging a bad situation is not the same thing as accepting it as final, giving up or assuming it's not there. It is! I've heard people say "You can fake it until you make it", and that you have to be strong or pretend. The problem is – you can fake it but never make it. Faking reality will even keep you in a weaker position.

It is very difficult to feel the need to act or to do something without acknowledging your situation. A person who was beaten twice, who says he has only been beaten once, is only wallowing in self-deception. It is one thing to be deceived by others and another thing entirely to deceive yourself. Self-deception brings temporary relief or makes others feel nothing serious has happened. It may cause delay in healing, truncate deliverance or abort a person's destiny. When people deceive themselves they focus only on what they want to focus on or what they want to believe. They deliberately ignore the evidence but the truth remains the truth, whatever the fact says. Tragically sometimes, someone in self-deception may hide from the person that God has sent to help them – a very sad position for anyone to be in.

You may already feel vulnerable, and you are very careful about who to open up to; but you must acknowledge to God what has happened. If you have missed it, messed it up or blown it, don't hide it from God. In fact He knows already; He only wants you to acknowledge and confess it. Being vulnerable in the hand of God can never be the worst thing that could happen to you. God is the one who has mercy and in whose hand you can be sure of deliverance. This is the way David put it when he received a judgement from God: "I am in great distress. Please let us fall into the hand of the LORD, for His mercies are great; but do not let me fall into the hand of man" (2 Samuel 24:14).

In Luke 18:41, Jesus asked the blind man, "What do you want Me to do for you?" The blind man did not beat about the bush; he gave a straightforward and honest answer: "Lord, that I may receive my sight." His sight was immediately restored. God knows about the situation already; He is only waiting for you to ask. Be true to yourself and to God; don't embark on a journey of self-deception.

I once saw in a dream a mighty eagle perched on a big tree. I could barely make out the tree branches due to the thick and dark green leaves. The eagle was unable to move from its position and I realised later that one of its wings was broken. I then saw a figure or something that looked like a hand moving the eagle to a higher level on the tree. As I have always done, I asked God for the meaning of what I saw in the dream. God impressed it upon my spirit that sometimes even a mighty eagle might find itself in a situation where it cannot help itself. It is the hand of God that strengthens the weary. You must not be filled with pride to the extent that you cannot be vulnerable in the hand of your maker. He has said in His word (Psalm 50:15): "Call upon Me in the day of trouble; I will deliver you, and you shall glorify Me."

Wait

Wait; and while you wait, take the weight off your mind. "Those that wait upon the Lord shall renew their strength and mount up with wings like eagles, they shall run and not be weary, they shall walk and not faint" (Isaiah 40:31). You become stronger when you wait and focus on God. The devil wants you to focus on the problem but God wants you to focus on Him. Waiting affords you the opportunity to meditate on the goodness of God in your life and the life of others around you. Your focus will be on God only if you meditate on who He is. Meditate on his mercies, for tangible and intangible things in your life – your health, your children, your parents, your job, your marriage, your family, your friends, your house, your neighbours, your employer and for those things that the devil wants to attack in your life. Remind yourself of the big and small battles that God has won on your behalf. Thank God for the things that the enemy has stolen which you were not even aware of, and for the restoration which you did not pray for.

Sometime around May 2000, I attended a revision course in London and returned home not realising that I had left my revision book at a train station. One day while at work, I was called to receive a parcel sent by one Adam, a man I have never met before. It was the book! I did not realise it was missing until I received the parcel. With the examination so close, I would have bought a replacement if I had known the book was gone. That would have set me back thirty pounds sterling. Adam was visiting London from Scotland and had posted the book back to me when he returned home. Adam even took time to enclose a letter which read: *"Rather amazingly I found this book on a bench, on a platform, in a station in South East London last month (I forget which one), while down visiting a friend. I thought it was a bit of good fortune on my part but on coming to leaf through it I noticed an invoice with your name and address on it. I am therefore returning it to you in the hope that you haven't bought a replacement in the meantime."* Thank God, I hadn't.

Praise Him and bless the Lord

Praise Him, praise Him and praise Him. Magnify the Lord in your heart all the time and don't let His praises cease from your mouth. Bless the Lord at all times, and don't stop praising him. The devil doesn't know what to do with someone who does not know how to stop praising God despite being in a difficult situation. That was what Paul and Silas did when they were thrown into prison. Magnify the goodness of God, and remember those things that he has done for you – the little and the big things. If creditors have taken away your house, thank God for keeping a roof over your head since then. It could have been worse – there are thousands of people living homeless on streets supposedly paved with gold. Thank God for when you crossed the road and you didn't get run over by a car. Thank Him for your good health, your job and for the people you have around you.

> My heart is steadfast O God, my heart is steadfast. I will sing and make music. I will praise you, O Lord, among the nations; I will sing of you among the peoples. For great is your love, reaching to the heavens; your faithfulness reaches to the skies. Be exalted, O God, above the heavens; let your glory be over all the earth. (Psalm 57:7–11)

Sing to Him a new song

I don't mean for you to learn a new song but to sing a different tune from what you have been singing. Rather than sing about all that is going wrong, sing to the Lord that He is your refuge and strength, and your help in the time of need. Sing to yourself, "It is Well with My Soul." Sing it again and again and mean it.

Horatio Spafford, a successful Christian lawyer and the author of this popular song was born on 20 October 1828 in North Troy, New York. He wrote this hymn after he suffered several calamities and traumatic events in his life. The music for "It is Well with My Soul" was later composed by Philip P. Bliss (1838–1876) who died in a tragic train accident shortly afterwards.

Spafford was deeply spiritual; he was devoted to the scriptures and engaged in several Christian activities. Spafford's devotion to God did not spare him darkness in his life; his only son died at the age of four. Spafford had a huge real estate investment wiped out following a fire in Chicago in 1871. Two years after the fire, Spafford planned a trip to Europe for his family and also wanted to support evangelism in Great Britain during that journey. Spafford had a last minute business transaction on the day they were due to depart, and stayed behind in Chicago. He sent his wife and four daughters to travel on the S.S. *Ville du Havre*. The plan was for him to follow them a few days later.

On 22 November, the ship carrying Spafford's wife and daughters collided with *Loch Earn*, an English vessel, and was sunk within minutes. Spafford learnt later that his wife had survived but his four daughters had drowned. Spafford left by ship to meet his grieving wife shortly after. While passing by where the tragedy occurred, he was inspired to write about his own personal grief – "When sorrows like sea billows roll ..." The hymn "It is Well with My Soul" was born. Despite those personal tragedies and sorrows, Spafford was able to say with very touching and such convincing clarity that "It is well with my soul." That song has ministered to countless souls the world over. I have reproduced the whole song on the next page to help you.

It is Well with My Soul

When peace like a river, attendeth my way,
When sorrows like sea billows roll;
Whatever my lot, Thou hast taught me to say,
It is well, it is well, with my soul.

Refrain:
It is well, with my soul,
It is well, with my soul,
It is well, it is well, with my soul.

Though Satan should buffet, though trials should come,
Let this blest assurance control,
That Christ has regarded my helpless estate,
And hath shed His own blood for my soul.

My sin, oh, the bliss of this glorious thought!
My sin, not in part but the whole,
Is nailed to the cross, and I bear it no more,
Praise the Lord, praise the Lord, O my soul!

For me, be it Christ, be it Christ hence to live:
If Jordan above me shall roll,
No pang shall be mine, for in death as in life,
Thou wilt whisper Thy peace to my soul.

But Lord, 'tis for Thee, for Thy coming we wait,
The sky, not the grave, is our goal;
Oh, trump of the angel! Oh, voice of the Lord!
Blessed hope, blessed rest of my soul.

And Lord, haste the day when my faith shall be sight,
The clouds be rolled back as a scroll;
The trump shall resound, and the Lord shall descend,
Even so, it is well with my soul.

Horatio Spafford (1828–1888)

Put your focus on Him

Put your focus on God when things are difficult. Thank God for your brother, your sister, friend, boss, in-laws and pastors who are all trying to help but be sure of one thing – they are not the source of your help – they are only useful instruments in the hand of God. As you wait for your breakthrough, focus your eyes on God. He may decide to use a man or a woman, a boy or a girl, a pauper or a rich man – that is down to Him. The true solution is in God and woe unto him that puts his trust in another man. Those who put their trust in God are like Mount Zion, which shall never be moved. When you face a difficult challenge, raise up your eyes unto God where your help comes from; put your attention on him one hundred percent. Like a camera, what you focus on is what you get in the picture. Whatever you focus on becomes bigger – if you focus on the problem, it gets bigger and if you focus on the promise, a solution comes your way.

Meditate on the word

You don't need to have a PhD in physics to understand the power of light over darkness – wherever light shows up, darkness disappears. The entrance of God's word is what gives light; it gives understanding to the simple. The word refreshes; brings revelation, deliverance, comfort and many more things. The scope of this book will not allow me to expand on the subject of the light and you will find extensive and more authoritative literature on the subject elsewhere. God's word is His light and the light of God is His word.

Most people will agree that when you are in darkness, the more natural preference is to want to come out. What you do, what you need and how you come out is something totally different. The Bible says in Psalm 119:105 that "Your word *is* a lamp to my feet And a light to my path." One day, I noticed something peculiar about this verse – it contains two pairs of

46

words – "lamp–feet" and "light–path". You have to be careful where you place your feet when you are in darkness, otherwise you might step on stones or other dangerous objects. You might also step on people's toes. What the word does is to light the lamp and the lamp is what illuminates where you should place your feet – I call this position. When you find yourself in a very dark situation, you are also looking for the way out, and more often than not, there is usually more than one way. The path is what leads to where you are going and the light of God's word shines in darkness to show you where God really wants you to be – I call this direction. You need position (or stance) and direction if you are to achieve good outcomes in matters of life, and the panacea (a word I rarely use) is the word of God. The word of God is Light and God Himself – eat it, drink it and breathe it. When you do, the darkness in your life will disappear.

Speak and confess the word

The word "confess" comes from the Latin word *confiteri* which means "to acknowledge" or "to say the same thing as". Use your mouth – speak to God, to yourself and to your situation. "Death and life are in the power of the tongue" (Proverbs 18:21); the words that you speak are spirit and they are life – speak them again and again.

You must develop a positive attitude, and speak to your soul like David did in Psalm 42:5 "Why are you cast down, O my soul and why are you in turmoil within me? Hope in God; for I shall again praise him, my salvation and my God." If you find yourself in a difficult place and don't know what to do, burn Romans 8:28 in your spirit – it says "And we know that all things work together for good to those who love God, to those who are the called according to His purpose." The affliction that you suffer presently is not comparable to the bigger glory that awaits you. All things will work together for good for those who love God and those that are called according to His purpose. What do I mean by this? I mean everything concerning where you are now will work together for good for you. Your mistakes, abandonment, maltreatment, frustration, annoyance, betrayal or irritation – they will all work together and God will use them to glorify Himself.

Pray

Prayer is the master key, the slender nerve that moves the hand of the Omnipotent. You may have wondered why I did not suggest prayer should be the first thing you do when you are in trouble. That was deliberate. When you are very distressed, you can pray emotional and automatic prayers that do not touch the ceiling. Sometimes you pray in fear and not in faith – that equally would not achieve the desired result. But seek the mind of God on what to pray about so that you don't pray amiss.

You must pray when you find yourself in a difficult place. This might sound straightforward, but you will be amazed to know the extent to which some people will go doing unnecessary and sometimes crazy things rather than pray when they are in trouble. I have seen people go about to plan, to ponder or to plot revenge instead of praying. Pray first; don't run here and there or leave prayer to the last minute to use as a spare part when everything else has failed. Pray at all times and without ceasing. God is saying don't stop praying until you see your breakthrough. This is clearly pointed out in the scriptures:

> I have set watchmen on your walls, O Jerusalem; They shall never hold their peace day or night. You who make mention of the LORD, do not keep silent, And give Him no rest till He establishes And till He makes Jerusalem a praise in the earth. (Isaiah 62:6–7)

If someone has hurt you very badly or put you in a difficult situation, don't think about never forgiving them. It might be difficult, but ask God to supply the grace to forgive those who have wronged you. Pray for strength to hold on; pray for God to help you and others in the situation with you, and for God to make way where there is no way. If you are going through a dark period caused by others, pray that God forgive them and use the situation that you are in for His glory. Pray that in the middle of your difficulties you will not deny God and that you will not lose your faith or your mind.

Countless materials exist on prayer and on how to pray; I'm certainly nowhere near being an authority on the subject. But God recently revealed to me an approach which I have found useful. I call it "My Seven Weapons of Warfare". These are nothing new and I have highlighted them below:

> The *Righteousness* of God – the devil would always want to point out to you and to God how bad or horrible you have been in your life, and how you are not worthy of what you are asking for. You will be held in bondage if you buy that lie. No man can be right on his own, and your righteousness which gives you boldness and right-standing is only given by God. And you have to take it by faith.

> The *Word* of God – the word of God is His will and this is what you have to use to establish the purpose and will of God for your life.

> The *Holy Spirit* of God – the Spirit of God knows the *hidden secrets* of God; He teaches you how to pray and what to pray about. The Holy Spirit is the *Enforcer*, the one that establishes the will of God on Earth.

> The *Name* of Jesus – this *Name* is higher than any other thing that has a name. It is yours if you are true child of God. At the mention of the *Name*, everything in life subjects to it.

> The *Blood* of Jesus – this is the bullet-proofing for life's adversity. The *Blood* has covered everything, and because the *Blood* has taken away sicknesses, hurt and pain, you don't have them any more.

The *Mercies* of God – the mercies of God bring His favour and you must ask for it. It is God's mercy that turns a pauper into a prince, and someone who is disillusioned into a deliverer. It's all yours for the asking.

The *Right Hand* of God – O I love it! This is the *Strength* of God; it penetrates rocks and mountains; it breaks bars of limitation into pieces; and nothing can withstand it. The *Right Hand* of God opens doors; it plucks out of darkness and brings full restoration. You and I need it!

I encourage you to ask God for wisdom on how to apply this seven-prong approach. I can tell you it works.

Ask God for direction

When you find yourself in a difficult place, ask God what you should do before you act. If you ask and listen, you will get an answer, usually communicated through your mind, your thoughts or your spirit. Hearing from God brings true understanding and wisdom about a particular situation. While David was in battle with the Philistines, Ziklag was raided by the Amalekites who burnt the whole town down. The invaders captured David's wives and children and the wives of his men and their children. On their return, the men were angry and wanted to stone David. To say David was confused and grieved would be an understatement – he tore his robes to show his distress. He then asked God what he should do before making a move. God told David to pursue the Amalekites, and he recovered all that was taken.

You need to hear clearly from God what to do because there is no shortage of advisers who are too willing to offer you their services for free. A person who is going through a dark period of life can be vulnerable and could listen to multitude of counsel – some counterproductive or even contradictory. These advisers may be people who are hurting or "wounded soldiers" who are still nursing their own wounds of adversity. Remember the phrase "hurt people hurt people" – it's very true indeed. These people are likely to offer you counsel purely out of their own experience, hurt and disappointment. It is important not to listen to everything that you hear from the multitude of advice that are trying to drown you. The best guarantee you could have is to hear from God. How? By asking and by listening.

Be continuously productive

Remember Joseph? He went from his father's house to the pit and from the pit to prison. Joseph suffered for 13 years because he held onto a God-given dream, and it got darker and darker for him. One would have thought that as life became more difficult for Joseph, he would become bitter and abandon his dream. Not Joseph; he kept on being productive and interpreting dreams – the very thing that got him into trouble in the first place. Eventually when he interpreted another dream, he was made a Prime Minister in a foreign land. God turned his darkness into destiny.

I have always believed there was something special about Joseph that made him hold onto his dream in the face of adversity. I have heard it preached several times that Joseph had an exceptional grace and an uncommon perspective which made him do what others would not do in the circumstances in which he found himself. I have listened to sermons on how "special" Joseph was concerning the dream and the mission that God gave him. I held this view until recently, while discussing Joseph at dinner with my wife and a pastor who was visiting. My wife blurted out, "There is nothing special about Joseph". I thought for a moment, and said: "What do you mean?" And I added, "No natural man would do anything close to what Joseph did."

My wife had done her homework, and she noticed I wasn't ready to give up. Then she added, "The only reason why Joseph did not give up his dream, enjoy illegitimate sex with Potiphar's wife, stop interpreting dreams or plot revenge against his brothers when they came to Egypt for food was that God was with Joseph." I thought that was preposterous; that couldn't be the only reason. I later looked closely at the account in the Bible – my wife was correct. I couldn't find anything else. It was recorded on four occasions that God was with Joseph (Genesis 39: verses 2, 3, 21 and 23) and that was what made the whole difference. To be honest, I had never seen it that way before. Joseph was only able to endure the challenges he faced not because he was a nice, strong-willed or a disciplined person; it was because God was with him.

"God is our refuge and strength, a very present help in trouble" (Psalm 46:1), and without Him we cannot do anything, no matter how much we wish we could. The Bible says in John 15:5: "I am the vine, you are the branches. He who abides in Me, and I in him, bears much fruit; for without Me you can do nothing." God who was with Joseph is with you today. If you are a born-again Christian and have given your life to Jesus, He lives inside you; you can do more exploits than Joseph did. You can have a comeback!

Don't be intimidated

Intimidation comes in various shapes and forms, and you must learn not to be intimidated when trouble rears its ugly head. When the devil wants to intimidate a deliverer, he leads the person into captivity. That was what happened to Samson. When the enemy wants to intimidate a doctor, the enemy inflicts his or her body with sickness. The devil will not shy away from sowing seeds of discontent in a congregation if his agenda is to intimidate the pastor and the elders. The devil will cause marital disharmony in the life of a marriage counsellor or divorce for a woman of God whose ministry is to deliver thousands of couples in troublesome marriages. When the enemy attacks anything in your life, be sure that is what the enemy is most afraid of about you. The enemy is afraid of you; refuse to be intimidated, and don't allow the devil to rubbish your testimony. The righteous may fall seven times but the righteous will rise again. I must urge you to stand firm on the word of God.

I will never forget one morning when I was praying and my phone rang just before 7:00am. Normally I wouldn't have answered the phone but I felt strongly pressed in my spirit to do so. A distressed voice came on the line and I recognised it immediately as that of a family friend. The devil had inflicted her son with a serious disease, and the boy had lost a year of university, most painfully in the final year! I knew about this already and had been praying along with the family. I strongly felt the need to pray again but the devil wanted to intimidate me. For a moment I asked myself which other prayer I was going to pray that had not been said already by the parents or that I had not prayed before myself. I however refused to be intimidated – I asked the lady to come over to my house that morning before I left for work.

While she was on her way, I quickly went on my computer and printed on two sheets of A4 size paper three passages of the Bible, which I intended to make real in the lives of our family friend and her son. The three passages are reproduced below:

The decision is announced by messengers, the holy ones declare the verdict, so that the living may know that the Most High is sovereign over the kingdoms of men and gives them to anyone he wishes and sets over them the lowliest of men. (Daniel 4:17, New International Version)

O our God, will You not judge them? For we have no power against this great multitude that is coming against us; nor do we know what to do, but our eyes are upon You. (2 Chronicles 20:12)

Behold, as the eyes of servants look to the hand of their masters, As the eyes of a maid to the hand of her mistress, So our eyes look to the LORD our God, Until He has mercy on us. (Psalm 123:2)

The Bible passages were to help our understanding of the situation. The laboratory and the doctors had sent a test result but I knew they were only messengers; God is the one that has the final say. I acknowledged the test result as a letter over which we had no power and declared that our eyes were on God. I acknowledged that I was helpless and declared my total dependence on Him.

Fortunately I had just finished a men's meeting at our church and had some anointing oil at home. The stage was set for battle and I was poised for a showdown with the enemy. The lady came into my living room very distressed, with the laboratory result in her hand. As a doctor, I knew why she was worried about the diagnostic report. At the same time I knew medical science has its limits, and that there is a God in Heaven who has no limits and who is the giver of medical knowledge itself. I made two copies of the laboratory result, and attached them to the passages of the Bible. I poured the anointing oil on the two copies, one for me and one for our family friend.

As we knelt down together to pray, I said, "You are a Christian and I don't need to tell you this, but I just want to re-emphasise that the only reason why we pray is that we have a God in heaven who answers prayers." I invoked the passages of the Bible as we prayed and we yanked the boy off the shackle of illness. I sent the lady away with the peace of God and an oil-soaked copy of the laboratory result attached to her copy of the Bible passages. I prayed on my own copies every day until I was reassured in my spirit. I was so sure that the devil had lost the battle. When the boy next visited the doctors they could not find anything wrong with him. God Almighty is the one who is able to do more than we can imagine, think or ask. The boy completed his degree course that year and went on to pursue a Masters degree. Don't be intimidated by the devil; take authority and stand on the word of God.

Magnify the goodness of God and praise him

I must not fail to consider the importance of magnifying the goodness of God and his bigness far above any problems you may be experiencing. Different people have different ways of doing this but the truth about praising God is the same – when you magnify God, He doesn't get bigger; He is already bigger than the biggest thing that ever existed. It is your perception of his awesomeness that gets bigger as you keep your focus on Him. One effective way to put your focus on God is to engage in praise and worship in the middle of adversity. It doesn't come to one naturally but it's a choice you must make.

Praise and worship are functions of your will and it is you who has to make the decision whether to praise God or not. The Psalmist once said, "I will magnify the Lord; His praises shall continually be in my mouth" (Psalms 34:1). Let me be honest with you, it can be very difficult to praise God in the middle of difficult, dark or dangerous situations, but praising God is a decision and not a feeling. And it doesn't have to be complex – you might find it useful to sing, dance or clap – it's up to you. The song "Who is Like Unto Thee Oh Lord?" is a good one to consider if you are going through a dark period and want to praise and worship God. I have reproduced this very simple song to help you sing it.

Who is Like Unto Three Oh Lord?

Who is like unto Thee Oh Lord(?) (4x)
Among the gods, who is like Thee?
Glorious in holiness
And fearful in praises
Always doing wonders
Hallelujah

I encourage you to sing this song with all forms of melody; in your understanding and in tongues (your spirit language), with music or without music. What you sing is your confession; you must sing it until it enters your spirit. If you have ever been anywhere near where clothes are dyed, you may find it easy to understand how this works. When a cloth maker puts a cloth in the dye bowl, there is a particular point in time when the cloth first touches the dye – this is when the cloth acknowledges a wish to acquire a new identity. Shortly after, the cloth fabric starts to absorb the dye and after a while the dye fastens itself onto the fabric. Even though it is still wet the cloth is already permanently dyed. At this point, whether you wash it with water or other liquids, the dye will not go away. The cloth and the dye have become one.

God is spirit and those that worship Him must worship Him in spirit and in truth. When you make a decision to sing the praises of God in your dark hour, you are at first operating in your head. As you begin to praise Him, you arouse forces in the heavenly realm. As you continue to do so, the praise moves from your head into your heart and from your heart into your spirit. The praise in your spirit is the one that identifies with the spirit of God, and that is when you can really commune with Him. There is no telling what shackles can be broken when your spirit communicates directly with God's spirit. Mountains of opposition will melt like wax in the presence of the Lord.

If you are not the type given to many words or you find the song above a bit too long, I encourage you to try a shorter but equally powerful song of praise – "You are High and Lifted Up." Again I have reproduced the whole song below in case you are not familiar with it.

You are High and Lifted Up

You are high and lifted up
There is no one like you
Halle, Halle, Halle, Hallelujah

Sing it again and again until it enters your spirit. The third line of this song has an unusual peculiarity; it is like fanning the flame at a blacksmith or a goldsmith's workshop. With the compression of the air bag each time comes the fanning of the flames, which become hotter and hotter. The fanning of the flame is essentially what melts the metal. "Halle, Halle, Halle" is the fanning that makes the flame hotter, and you will notice that the third "Halle" has the highest pitch of the three. You can say that it is the hottest flame that finally melts the metal. The third "Halle" with the highest pitch (the hottest) is followed by "Hallelujah" with a softer pitch, suggesting a release and a melting away of the difficult situation. This is the point when the mountain in your life starts to melt like wax before the presence of the Lord.

Sing "You are high and lifted up" until it moves from your head into your heart and into your spirit. In fact sing any song that comes to mind. Move the praise from your head into your heart, and move it from your heart into your spirit. Sing His praises aloud or sing in the quietness of your spirit. Continue to sing your song of deliverance even if no word comes out of your mouth. Magnify Him above all the Earth, above the Heavens and above all your problems. As you do this, God becomes infinitesimally big and awesome and your problems become infinitesimally small and tiny. Something will shift in the heavenly realm and your breakthrough will come.

God is saying hold your ground even when it looks as if it's going from bad to worse. It's already bad when the earth gives way when you are involved in an earthquake or when you are going through challenges of seismic proportions. It's even worse when the mountain of opposition and obstacle is thrown into the sea. At this point the sea is bound to overflow the shores with potential for flooding, drowning and destruction. This is the point when a person might feel overwhelmed and want to give up. In the middle of all this, you should say to yourself "I will not fear." God, you must know, has not given you the spirit of fear, but of power and of love, and a sound mind (2 Timothy 1:7).

Prepare to come out

The dark period of life is not your final destination and you must prepare to come out. Always think about victory. Your corresponding action is what shows whether you are preparing to come out or not. When the prodigal son (Luke 15:11–15) squandered his inheritance in a far country, he landed a job where he had to feed pigs. He had nothing and would gladly have eaten the food meant for the pigs if that was offered to him. The problem was that no one offered him anything, not even the leftovers from the pigs' food. One day, the prodigal son said to himself: "Enough is enough." He realised he had messed up greatly but again thought to himself that even servants in his father's household didn't have to go hungry – they had food to eat. The prodigal son made a very crucial decision and said "I will arise." And arise he did. Otherwise, the prodigal son would have stayed in that miserable position for the rest of his life.

You need to make adequate preparation if you want to come out of darkness. I previously worked with drug addicts who were hooked on illegal drugs such as cocaine, crack and heroin. I will never forget a gentleman who was making a great effort to stop using cocaine which he used to snort and sometimes smoke. I saw him in my clinic weekly and I was glad he was making good progress. He made a considerable effort to clean up his act and he avoided all his drug-using friends and the drug dealers. These so-called friends knew the easiest way to lure him back was to post another "free" sample of cocaine through his letterbox. One day he came into my clinic very tearful before his next appointment. Cruelly, the drug dealers had posted some cocaine powder through his door that morning and he could not resist the temptation. Bang – he was back on drugs!

While I was still trying to work out what to say to him, the gentleman blurted out: "Doctor I know you must really be disappointed in me. I have however decided to move out of this area for now and form more positive relationships elsewhere." The man knew that his chances of giving up illegal drugs were next to nothing as long as he continued to hang out with his drug-using friends and live in an area which was riddled with crack, cocaine and heroin. He prepared to come out of that horrible situation; he moved out of the area and we supported him. Many years later he was free from drugs. He now has a good job and looks after his family.

Let me remind you of the story of the Chilean miners once again. As soon as the miners realised they were trapped, and before they managed to make contact with the outside world, they decided they were going to keep busy. They were not busy digging their own graves or sending farewell messages to their families. The very religious among them were not saying their last rites or giving last rites to the less religious. There was no account of anyone saying "from earth we came and to the earth we shall return, blessed be the name of the Lord". No, not the Chilean miners – they acted in ways that portrayed their intention, which was to come out alive to tell their stories. Some were busy writing their diaries or memoirs, and some were looking for rock souvenirs to give to families and friends. Some were already planning how to sell their story and others were planning how they would handle the pressure which their new-found celebrity status might bring. All their actions showed that their intention was to come out alive.

Under the leadership of 54-year-old Liuz Urzua who was the shift commander at the time of the disaster, the miners divided themselves into groups to do shifts, and to keep fit. The men took tiny sips of milk and a bite of tuna fish every other day and managed to stretch food meant for 48 hours for 17 days. You must realise that while they were doing all this, they hadn't even made any contact with the outside world. The miners had strong faith that somehow, someone somewhere would come looking for them. It didn't matter to them whether their rescuers were from their company, the Chilean government or experts from the United States NASA programme. As far as they were concerned, they were coming out. That's the mindset anyone in trouble should have no matter how difficult or hopeless the situation might seem.

The devil wants you to stay in dark and dingy places but you must prepare to come out. You must do exactly the opposite of what the enemy wants you to do. Prepare the way for the Lord, make room for God in your life, have a vessel ready for your blessings, increase your capacity, build the broken altars in your life and repair the cracks in your relationships. Change your garments; literally and spiritually. When Joseph interpreted the dream that took him to the palace, he changed from prison clothes to more befitting garments. When Jesus arose from the grave, He abandoned the grave clothes and walked away. When Jesus raised Lazarus from death, He told His disciples to "Loose him and let him go." The embalming cloth was taken away from Lazarus to prepare him for his new life. As you prepare to embrace your new beginning, change your garment, change your mindset, change your thinking and change your life. Prepare to come out; do something different today.

8

Looking In The Wrong Places

During my many years of meeting people from different racial, religious, cultural and socio-economic backgrounds, I am yet to come across anyone who does not believe God can help them out of their difficult situation. Many can even tell you how they believe their breakthrough will come and are willing to follow God's lead for the solution. However, what many have done is to figure God out on what He is going to do or who He is going to send or use to bring about their much-needed deliverance. They are looking towards their parents, friends, husband, doctor, lawyer, pastor, college, government or charitable organisations to come to their aid; and nothing is particularly wrong with that. The problem usually is that when people plan to come out of a bad situation, they work everything out very neatly in their minds but leave God out of the equation. Society, secular humanism and the DIY (do-it-yourself) culture are all saying the same thing – "There is no God"; "You are the master of your own destiny"; "It's your life" or "Do whatever pleases you". Something is definitely wrong with this.

Don't get me wrong; God sometimes uses people to accomplish His purpose on Earth but He works things out according to His own plan and agenda. God doesn't do things the way a man does or wants (Isaiah 55:8). When you think you have figured God out and He doesn't come through for you the way you had expected, you become easily frustrated and disappointed. This is what happened to me when I passed through some very dark periods in my own life. My situation may not seem dark enough, and I may not have passed through the same journey as yours, but be clear of one thing – the dark periods in my life were no less important, less difficult or less frightening than yours. I believe you can learn one thing or another from my account.

You read earlier about my remarkable birth and how I had four mothers when I was growing up. I was born two days after my "twin" brother, Abbey, and my step-mother told me at the age of 11 that she was not my biological mother. I was left defenceless when my step-mother died shortly afterwards. My father "adopted" several other children in addition to having many of his own. As the children grew up and we increased in number, the house became busier and noisier. Polygamy took its toll, and it became more difficult to read, concentrate, focus on my studies or plan for the future while living in my father's house. I knew clearly I had to do something quickly and at that point I moved to live with my father's older sister. Staying with my older aunt who was a strict disciplinarian and a Christian set me on a good path and I found a good role model in my cousin, Sam. Although we are cousins, I called him my brother all the time, and most people who knew us thought of us as such.

Sam and my other cousins were brought up single-handedly by my aunt with occasional support from my father. Their father died when they were very young. Sam and his older brother took up all sorts of jobs to make ends meet and to provide for the family. I still remember clearly how Sam constantly used to say, "Mooyee [as I was called then], you cannot afford to fail." Sam knew what he was talking about and had seen a lot himself. Sam struggled financially through university and sold artworks to earn some money. It grieved me to see Sam sell one of his prized possessions – a very expensive wristwatch – for forty Naira – the equivalent of three British pounds at the time. He needed the money for transport to return to university to sit his final examination. Otherwise that would have been the end of his four-year university education.

I was approaching my fourth year at medical school and Sam

had set his eyes on travelling abroard after he completed his degree course. Not surprisingly, money was the problem. Fortunately, I won a Mobil Oil Producing scholarship of 2,000 Naira (about £155) and I gave Sam 1,400 Naira towards his travel. I was very happy for him and we held a meeting at my students' hostel bedroom before Sam travelled. We both worked it out that once Sam settled down abroad, he would send for me and his brother. The plan was going to work out fine and no one could convince me otherwise.

Sam travelled out of Nigeria and called the next day from London. We were all happy that Sam landed safely and that shortly after, he started doing well (as we thought). He paid my money back and even bought a pair of shoes for my girlfriend who is now my wife. As planned, and after about two years, Sam sent for his brother who later joined him in England. Sadly, my aunt, Sam's mother, died in August 1991 after a protracted illness. I developed cold feet about travelling after Sam's mother died – another defence was gone from me forever! The idea of abandoning medical school in the fifth year did not appeal much to me and I decided it was better to graduate as a doctor first before looking for greener pastures elsewhere. And then everything went silent – I did not hear much from Sam again for six years!

I qualified as a doctor in 1992, a time of political turmoil in Nigeria. The ruling military government at the time had just annulled a free and fair presidential election. Pandemonium had broken out; more professors and established senior doctors left the country to seek lucrative contracts in the Middle East. As a very junior doctor then, I had no chance. Everyone who could travel abroad did. If there was any time I needed my brother Sam to help, it was then. I had lost contact with him for the better part of six years. I was desperate, and felt stuck too.

What did I do wrong? Did Sam hear something bad about me? Did he think I would become a burden to him? Did Sam's mother (my aunt and my fourth mother) say something to him to make him forget about all our plans? Several questions went through my mind but I had no answer. Why me? And why Sam of all people? The same Sam had woken me up every day to teach me mathematics, physics and chemistry in the summer of 1984. It was the same Sam that paid the fee for an additional subject for my GCSE to make sure I had five 'O' level subjects to enter university in 1985. Sam was the one that kept on ringing in my ears: *"Mooyee, you can't afford to fail."* How on earth could he abandon me just like that when I needed him most? Why, why and why? I could not understand.

Without the necessary financial resources and support, I settled for the one-year national youth service in Kebbi State in the northern part of Nigeria. By the time I returned to Lagos after my national service, everyone who could travel abroad had left. Many highly skilled professionals emigrated to Saudi Arabia, South Africa, Kenya, Ghana, the United States and the United Kingdom. The list was endless; in fact anywhere, as long as they did not stay at home. Many went abroad for postgraduate studies; many didn't even know what they were going abroad for. After a hard and long reflection, I said to myself, *"I am the only one left here; God, you have abandoned me."* Many years later, I asked God for forgiveness for that very stupid statement.

I began a frantic effort to travel abroad for postgraduate training or for anything else as long as I did not stay in a country engulfed in political turmoil, in a nation destabilised by industrial action and a society plagued with long queues for fuel. Social and political insecurity and the arrest of political opponents of the government had become daily national affairs. Hoodlums became kings and fraudsters emerged as champions in the celebrity arena. There was no need for anyone to join a gym at the time as there was enough exercise during the day jumping through bus windows or hatchbacks to get to work. You really had to master the art of catching a moving bus if you wanted to get home from work. I had three jobs, mainly to pay for the exorbitant rent in Lagos, the former capital city. I could not buy a decent T-shirt at the end of the month despite all my hard work.

At one time, I squatted with a friend alongside my wife who was two months pregnant with our first child. In addition to her morning sickness, my wife endured sleeping on a wooden bed with a mattress barely five centimetres thick. To put it simply, life was very hard. When our daughter Omowonuola was born, we named her after a very nice female classmate of mine whose name meant, "A child has entered into wealth". Our situation was nowhere near wealth. I will call it "survival" to be generous. On a few occasions, Ajay, a colleague of mine, had to lend me money to buy formula feed for my baby daughter when my salary was delayed, as it regularly was. You were lucky if your employer paid your salary by the tenth day of the month, and you still had to go to work or else you would have breached the terms of your contract. What contract you might ask?

My daughter Omowonuola enjoyed (or endured) lullabies sung by mosquitoes looking for blood meals at night. The mosquitoes had unhindered access to their dinner as most people had to sleep almost naked due to the intense heat, limited ventilation and very dismal electricity supply. There were constant disruptions in electricity supply for weeks if not months. It was a very dark period in our lives.

I was troubled and restless. I cried on my hospital clinic table and said: "God you have forgotten me here." My fear was real – I saw many people with great potential rot away due to lack of opportunities. I didn't want to end up like one of them. I applied for a visa to everywhere for anything in order to leave the country. I spent my salary sending UPS or DHL courier letters all over the world as the almost non-existent national postal service in Nigeria at that time couldn't be relied upon. Thank God for my prayerful wife who encouraged us to attend prayer meetings at The Redemption Camp near Lagos. My "Amen" was the loudest when Pastor Adeboye, the General Overseer of the Redeemed Christian Church of God used his trademark sentence: "There is somebody here who is going to receive a miracle." I prayed "like no man's business" as if my entire life depended on it. And it did, no kidding!

I was eventually granted a visa to Ireland but I could not find money for a flight ticket and the basic travel allowance (BTA). It was like a *déjà vu*. Two years before, one of my friends who studied physiotherapy had secured a visa to the United States, and for eight months, he couldn't raise enough money to travel. I clearly remembered saying at the time, "Not me; that's not possible. How can someone get a visa to God's own country and not have money to travel? Not me; that will never happen to me." That was exactly what happened to me – I had a visa but no money to travel to Ireland. That experience has taught me to be careful about my response when I see people going through difficulties in their lives.

You only really know who your friends are when you are in deep trouble or have a need. I had lost contact with my brother Sam and the other people I had banked on failed me spectacularly. Some of them couldn't even help themselves, not to talk of helping someone with a luxurious ambition of travelling abroad. I was looking in the wrong places. I worked harder and harder but there was only so much I could save when salaries did not come on time as expected. To say it was tough would be an understatement – it was really hard.

I knew I had to act fast. I sold all my medical equipment – white coats, surgical instruments, theatre boots and anything I could lay my hands on in order to raise money. I was offered ridiculous prices for my prized possessions and I convinced myself I had no choice and sold them. The most painful of all was selling the television that I bought for my wife when she was a student, something I knew she had very fond memories of. That is what happens in the dark hours of life – you rationalise things that should not be. I swallowed my pride and persuaded my wife for us to sell the television. I remember arguing at the time that it was better for us and our daughter to sell the TV to raise money so I could travel rather than for the three of us to get stuck in a rented flat with a TV without electricity.

I could not sell my car despite knocking half the price off. For most people at that time, there was no point in buying a car when you had to learn karate in order to buy fuel at petrol stations. Apart from that, the roads were not motorable. In all this, God was at work; I just didn't know it. I had my plans but God had His own plans. He raised help for me, some from where I never expected. I raised about eighty percent of the travel fare and the owner of the travel agent, a very nice Christian lady, agreed for my wife to pay the balance once my car was sold after I had gone. I was not even sure if the car was ever going to sell.

It was time to leave for Dublin. Emotions were so thick in the air you could cut them with a knife. I had to leave a young wife at home in the middle of political upheaval, uncertainty and lack. Our four-month-old daughter who was fast asleep when I was leaving had no say and did not bargain for any of that. My wife was not even sure whether I was ever going to come back for them or not. My wife and I used to talk about one of her cousins who had left for England years before and had never returned to marry his fiancée. The lady later married someone else after waiting for many years. That was not the time to remind my wife of such horror stories. My wife's favourite phrase "It is well" became more frequent as the time to depart drew near. "It is well", I said too, repeatedly. I believe my wife was anxious about what was going to happen in the following few months but she wouldn't admit it. She eventually consoled herself that the move was to make our situation better. She couldn't do anything else; it could only be for our good.

I packed all my credentials and a few belongings into my wife's old red travel bag. That was the same bag she had carried her belongings in when she started university seven years before. I bid my family and few friends goodbye and left for the airport. I changed my remaining local currency into about £17 at the airport and made for the check-in desk. To my surprise I didn't know I had to pay airport tax. The remaining £17 which was for my basic travel allowance (BTA) wasn't enough to cover that. I watched helplessly as my colleague Andrew and two other doctors travelling on the same flight checked in. I prayed earnestly for a miracle. I was looking for help in the wrong place and I waited to see if the check-in counter clerk would change her mind. I asked God to intervene and to use the clerk to waive the airport tax. God did not answer that prayer.

The plane left for Dublin that night without me. I couldn't travel without paying the airport tax. I was so disappointed! As sophisticated as I thought I was, I did not know about the airport tax until the last minute. I could not remember paying one when I went to Ghana three years before. The only thing I could do was to return home. A heavy sense of quietness and darkness descended as I left the airport with my luggage. I was more worried about what I would tell my wife was the reason why I could not travel that night. To my amazement, my wife was not as shocked as I had expected. Maybe she shed a few tears; that was all it was, I cannot remember clearly. I suspected she secretly felt a sense of relief and at the same time disappointment. I too was not sure whether I was relieved to be home with my family. I cannot recollect what happened or what we discussed that night as we fell asleep.

I woke up the next day to a bright Sunday morning but nothing had changed in our situation. Things might have got even worse if my ticket was no longer valid for travel. I could have lost close to 100,000 Naira, which was about a five-month salary for a young doctor at the time. I also owed the travel agent a balance of 15,000 Naira. The future looked bleak. I knew God had to come into my situation that day or else that would be it – my European dream would have vanished into thin air just like that. To my amazement, the airline confirmed they would still allow me to travel with the same ticket on Sunday evening as long as I paid the airport tax. The travel agent assistant told me that that was a miracle!

The second miracle followed soon afterwards. In the space of eighteen hours, someone had offered to buy my car which I had parked for nine months. I was offered one fifth of the money as down payment and the buyer promised to pay my wife the remaining money over the next four months. With one fifth down payment on the car, I had enough money for the airport tax and left the rest for my wife as a lifeline to keep my family going for a while. I changed the remaining money into British pounds sterling and I headed for Dublin with an impressive £33 travel allowance. I left for the airport that Sunday evening armed with my elusive airport tax fully paid. This time around I was more confident I would board the plane.

9

Flying Into The Unknown

I arrived at the Murtala Muhammed International Airport in Lagos at around four in the afternoon even though my flight was due to take off shortly after eleven at night. I had heard all sorts of stories before, and my travel had already been delayed the previous day. I couldn't afford for anything to go wrong. I dragged my bag through the crowd occupying the terminal building, and through several businessmen and women selling all sorts of things, including foreign currencies. With the ever- teeming crowd, you would be forgiven for thinking that the whole country was leaving their homeland for greener pastures. After going through all the formalities, I checked in my bag and waited for another four hours before we could board the plane where I was seated by a window in an economy class cabin. The plane taxied for a few minutes and we were airborne shortly afterwards.

I had just flown into the unknown. I thought to myself, "Now I am on my own." I felt lost with so many things going on in my mind. The situation was dark and even more so when I looked out through the cabin window. The aeroplane was surrounded by a thick dark sky. What gave me the assurance I was on the plane that dark night were the flickers of red light on the wings of the aircraft. I later heard a voice which said, *"Now you are on your own."* I thought that it was the devil, but again I felt that it was true. I was on my own with my wife and four-month-old daughter at home. I was on my own with only £33 travel allowance, not sure where I was going to stay on my arrival in Dublin. I tried to read magazines to distract myself but I couldn't concentrate. I kept on thinking I was on my own until a voice came through and said, *"No, you're not, I will be with you even till the end of age."* I knew that that was God.

I arrived in Dublin on the morning of Monday 27 January 1997. I was greeted at Immigration by a very nice middle-aged gentleman. "How long are you staying in Ireland?" he asked. "Two weeks or so," I replied. I told him that once I finished the first part of the membership examination of the Royal College of Physicians of Ireland, I would spend a week or two exploring pursuing postgraduate training in Ireland or in the UK. The officer put a stamp on my passport and passed me through. What a relief! I took a taxi to Avalon House, a bed and breakfast accommodation near Dublin town centre, a journey that set me back about seven Irish pounds. I had to watch every penny I spent given the amount of money I had with me. I paid £12 to stay for one night and was left with only £14 to survive in a foreign country. Worse still, I hadn't even spent a whole day there. Call it stupid or foolish – you are likely to be correct.

I moved in with Andrew and three other doctors the next day. It was not until I met Andrew that I realised how God had used the airport tax to delay my journey. It was a miracle, and the third one in three days! Andrew and the other colleagues who travelled a day before me (the day I returned home due to not having the airport tax) were all granted two weeks to stay in Ireland. I later discovered I was the only one granted six weeks' stay in Ireland when I came in on Monday morning. I had only £10 left but I had time and God on my side.

Andrew and the other colleagues with two-week visas on their passports started making plans to leave Ireland to avoid overstaying their time limits. The short tenancy on the flat that we shared was going to run out a day or two after their departure and I had no money to renew the rent and so had to leave. Andrew and the other guys were very generous; they gave me about £20 and left me some canned baked beans. However I too had to leave as

Andrew had to hand in the keys of the flat to the landlord in order to get a refund of his deposit. The problem was there was nowhere for me to go. Bryan, another colleague who I had met at the library, and who had promised to help, was not contactable. I found out later that Bryan was actually staying with a friend of someone who was also a lodger with another person. It was both a complicated arrangement and a hopeless situation – there was no point banking on that at all.

Somehow, I felt calm initially. I even saw Andrew off at the station as he headed for London. To my surprise, I ended up on the streets of Dublin with nowhere to go and nowhere to sleep that night. Given that pathetic situation, the more natural thing for me to do was to head for Dublin Airport and return to Nigeria straight away. I couldn't, and that wasn't even an option at all as I had sent back my return ticket home for my wife to cash. It quickly dawned on me that I was stuck – with only £20 and two or three cans of baked beans. My breathing became deeper and faster.

When I left home for Europe in January 1997, I had prepared myself for hard times but what I did not prepare for was that someone like me, a qualified medical doctor, a responsible family man and a free citizen of his own country, would find himself stranded on the streets of a foreign land. You could say I was naïve given the pathetic situation I faced before I left my country. It was like a scene from the television documentary series "An Idiot Abroad".

Whatever you think of the reality of my situation then, I was effectively stranded on the streets of Dublin. I couldn't even get a bed and breakfast hostel to stay the night in as everywhere was booked up. Revellers from all parts of Ireland and Europe had poured into Dublin for the weekend to enjoy their Guinness Stout on the banks of River Liffey. I was warned that the *Gardai* (Irish police) are not very nice people when it comes to illegal immigrants or overstayers. I did not belong to any of these categories, I thought to myself. In the true sense of the matter, I was neither an illegal immigrant nor an overstayer, but with no money, accommodation or means of sustenance, I was not different from hundreds of thousands of illegal immigrants or overstayers stranded on the streets in foreign lands all over the world. *"Where is God in all this?"* I asked. *"Now I am really on my own."* I needed no other proof!

It became darker and darker in the winter cold. The wind too was relentless and punishing. In desperation, I made a frantic call to a senior doctor colleague whom I had met earlier when I attended a church in Dublin. The doctor's wife was one of the midwifery students who came for training on the labour ward at the University College Hospital, Ibadan, Nigeria when I first qualified as a doctor. I remembered assisting the student midwives "to catch babies" (take deliveries) on the labour ward at the time – it was fun. My situation on the streets of Dublin that day was no fun at all. The senior doctor colleague either had "to catch a doctor" that day or the *Gardai* would do the catching.

Even though the senior colleague offered to pay for my accommodation for a few days, everywhere was booked up. The bed and breakfast accommodation managers were completely oblivious to my desperate situation. The hoteliers asked me to call back on Monday morning when the merry makers would have left Dublin. "Call back on Monday?" I queried. They must be joking! My priority was to find somewhere to stay between Friday night and Monday morning and none was forthcoming. All the accommodation in nearby towns was fully occupied. I was again warned that the threat of the *Gardai* was real. My bravado and initial calmness started to melt away.

As I couldn't find a place to stay in Dublin over that weekend, the only option left for me was to board a train to Naas (about 31 kilometres away and just over an hour by train) to stay with the doctor and his wife. My would-be hosts were concerned about the impact the distance would have on my studies in Dublin but were trying to persuade me about their offer. I knew I did not require any persuasion, and I quickly grabbed the lifeline. "Tomorrow can always take care of itself," I concluded. The next thing I knew I was on a train to Naas, on a cold windy night, weighted down by a heavy winter jacket given to me by George, another colleague who was almost twice my height. After one hour on the train, I made a less than ceremonious entry into Naas, a small town that was my home for two weeks or so.

I was picked up at the train station by my hosts who had also prepared a very hot meal for me. I tucked into the chicken and a traditional meal (*eba*) which I had not eaten for weeks. I felt homesick for the first time but I knew that this was not the time to be childish. I had to be strong for myself, my wife and my daughter. There was also a "great cloud of witnesses" out there waiting for me to make it. I knew I really had to be strong. The kindness and generosity of my hosts knew no bounds. I thanked them profusely and let them know how grateful I was for their unusual and kind gestures. My "thank yous" became too much for my hosts to bear and they begged me to "stop it". We went down memory lane and talked about how horrified student midwives who were coming to the labour ward for the first time used to "catch babies" in those days. We laughed and laughed. The last time I remembered laughing like that was when I was squatting with four other doctors in a cramped ground floor flat on the South Circular Road in Dublin. I even watched CNN and Sky News that night before I slept.

My hosts left for work early the next morning, and I had plenty of time to watch the news on television. I was so pleased to know that the *Gardai* had not been looking for a black man dragging a red bag around the city centre the day before. I reflected on how I had almost had an encounter with the *Gardai*. I journeyed between Naas and Dublin for about two weeks to explore furthering my career in Obstetrics and Gynaecology in the United Kingdom. A renowned professor of medicine had offered me a six-week clinical attachment to enable me to familiarise myself with the European system. Amazingly, when I couldn't return to Naas due to clinical commitments, the hospital arranged overnight accommodation and dinner for me. God was definitely at work.

I was eventually granted a visa to Britain with the assistance and guidance of my hosts. The time to leave Dublin had finally come. God had dealt so wondrously with me and I thanked Him. I was not surprised at all when a friend of my hosts who was also going back to England offered to pay my fare on the Irish Ferries. My faith in the Lord was back again, and things were happening so fast. Suddenly, I did not feel alone anymore.

I travelled back to Dublin after bidding my hosts an emotional farewell and arrived at the bus station in the city centre late in the afternoon. I showed my ticket to the inspector as I went through a small barrier. The inspector looked at the ticket for about twenty seconds and said something to one of his colleagues. Only God knows what they were discussing and I hoped they were not talking about the *Gardai*. I noticed I had become tense and my heart was beating faster. I managed to hide my anxiety and distracted myself by fiddling with the zip on my bag. *"Nothing must go wrong here,"* I prayed quietly. After checking and re-checking my ticket, the inspector said to me in a quiet and friendly voice, "Have a safe journey, see you back in Dublin soon." I thought to myself, *"You must be joking!"* and muttered a very sharp "Thank you."

I loaded my red bag on the bus and we made a very short journey through the town to the ferry port. The journey between Dublin ferry port and Holyhead on the English side was fairly turbulent due to high winds on the Irish Sea. I went out on the deck for a while to enjoy the scenery but there wasn't much to see. It was pitch dark except for the lights on the other ferry boats crossing the Irish Sea in the other direction. The thought of being alone wanted to come back to me again but I resisted it. Otherwise the entire journey across the Irish Sea was uneventful.

I travelled on a bus overnight and reached London Victoria on a Sunday morning. *"London, here I come,"* I grinned excitedly. I made straight for Walthamstow in the north-east of London to meet one of my classmates who had offered me accommodation. He was in church at the time and I quickly blended into the congregation as the church service was in full gear when I arrived. I saw a few eyes glance towards the back where I was sitting; they were mostly old classmates and their partners. I was obviously noticeable with my red bag at the back of the church hall and my heavy-duty jacket that resembled a Roman soldier's battle gear. I winked and nodded to acknowledge their greetings. *"The eagle has landed,"* they must have thought.

As soon as the church service finished, I was surrounded by a few old classmates who were attending the same church. Many were keen to see me and asked for news about home. I told them I had left Nigeria for about two months and that they needed to watch the BBC or CNN for current news items. That very day, without any application form, interview or a formal induction, I appointed myself as an usher in the church. I had promised God that if He made it possible for me to step on English soil, I would serve Him with all I had – I wasn't going to mess around with that promise. The senior minister in the church, Pastor Edward Adeagbo and his wife were very nice people, and they would often invite me and others to their house for lunch after services. The pastor also gave me one of his sharp sleek suits which almost became my uniform before I could afford new ones.

10

No Apologies

Following my arrival in London at the beginning of March 1997, I stayed with one of my classmates from medical school. At long last I had become a Londoner, but it came with a price. Pronouncing Woolwich in south-east London 'Wool Witch' raised many eyebrows before someone was kind enough to correct me that it is pronounced "wu-lidge". I once visited two of my colleagues in Greenwich (not "Green Witch") and one of them asked me if I liked apples. I responded by biting into one of the apples in front of me and was half-way into the second fruit when the other colleague reminded me that the question had been – "Do you like apples?" I knew straightaway I was caught out there! I ventured into the London Underground train network one day and ended up on the Circle Line. I only realised that the line was meant to go round in circles after spending three hours on the train. It took me more than a year to master the Circle Line and I took consolation in the fact that I was not the only person to have a similar experience.

I later joined a group of colleagues at London Southbank University to prepare for the PLAB medical licensing examination. That was after I sat the IELTS test to assess that my English was sufficient to safely practise medicine in Britain. This was despite being from a Commonwealth country and having studied all my life in the English language. Ironically a European Union (EU) national, for example a German doctor who has never spoken English before, whether qualified in the EU or not, does not have to sit the English test. I couldn't complain, and even if I did, no one was going to listen – I had asked for it.

Some time in May 1997, I bumped into one of my brother's friends at London Waterloo station. This was somebody I knew very well and someone who had been part of "the struggle". Steve offered his condolences for my aunt (Sam's mother) who had gone to be with the Lord in 1991. Steve was very excited and at the same time surprised to see me. He was even more surprised and did not initially believe me when I told him that I had no knowledge of where my brother Sam was. I told Steve that Sam probably had no clue I was in London. "Impossible," shouted Steve, not minding who else was around. Steve immediately tapped into his phone to call Sam but could not connect on his mobile and left a message for him. He gave me Sam's number and squeezed a £10 note into my hand for transport as he dashed off to work. I thanked God for the £10 gift. Clearly Steve had not forgotten his manners or his heritage, I thought.

Armed with Sam's mobile phone number and that of Steve, it was just a matter of time before I would see Sam. My heart was thumping over the prospect of meeting my brother again and I rehearsed in my mind again and again the questions I would ask Sam when I saw him. I thought about how I would express how disappointed I was about Sam abandoning me despite all I did for him and how I cared for his mother (my aunt who was my fourth mother) when Sam was away. I even thought carefully about how I would respond when Sam started to apologise for his misdeeds. *"Sam has to atone for his sins somehow,"* I thought to myself. Surely it would be a glorious time; I shook my head and rubbed my hands with glee.

By the time I got home that evening, Sam had called the house where I was staying and promised to call back later in the evening. His friend Steve, whom I met at Waterloo earlier in the day, had passed on my landlord's number to him as I did not have a mobile phone at the time. It was a long wait before 9:37pm when Sam eventually rang. We were both speechless for a few seconds, and were like strangers. That wasn't the Sam I knew before. Then I later heard the familiar voice, "Mooyee." I said, "Sam, long time." Sam replied, "How is everything?" I gave the natural answer, "Fine," knowing very well that everything was not fine between us, at least as far as I was concerned.

I had made up my mind I would not say much to Sam until we meet face-to-face. I wanted to give him a piece of my mind and tell him how disappointed I was, and also to allow him to give his unreserved and full apologies. Little did I realise the shock that was awaiting me! Sam invited me to his place over the weekend and we spoke on the phone a few times before we finally met. I travelled to meet Sam and his family in north London and it was an emotional reunion for me and for him. We drove about a mile from Edgware tube station to his house. I really cannot remember what we talked about before I settled down in his living room. We exchanged a few pleasantries and I hugged his wife and two daughters. I was surprised that Sam's little princesses had not even heard much about me. I took it as "one of those things" – and I can live with that.

I was left alone with Sam after we had dinner. My much-awaited opportunity to tell him how I felt about my abandonment finally came. I summoned courage and I asked Sam a very bold question and said, "Sam, how on Earth could you forget me just like that?" That was very bold! In African culture, you don't ask your older brother or someone older than you questions like that! The emotional apologies I had been waiting years for did not come. I was dumbfounded when Sam replied, "May God never forget any one of us." What? I was not sure whether that was a prayer or a comment. Was that all Sam had to say? Thinking Sam had not heard me properly, I repeated my question again but that was all Sam had to offer. I pressed him a bit harder, and Sam slightly improved on his answer: "It's not like that; as I said, may God never forget any one of us."

I was furious. I cannot remember Sam apologising at any time. I gave up when I knew the apology I was awaiting might never come. I decided to forgive and forget; after all, Sam is my brother. I might have become rude to Sam if I had persisted – that's very unlike Africans, and the occasion did not even call for that. I later asked myself: *"What exactly did Sam have to apologise for?"* I couldn't give a straightforward answer myself or pinpoint exactly what Sam had done wrong. Yes, I assisted Sam financially when he was travelling abroad, but he paid all my money back fully, and with interest, and also in kind, before we lost contact.

I decided to forget about it; but I couldn't. As I slept that night in Sam's house, I could not get myself away from it. What Sam said – "May God never forget any one of us" – kept on ringing in my ears throughout the night. It was much later after I had pondered over our reunion and how I found myself in Sam's house that I started connecting with what Sam actually said. It later occurred to me that anyone can be forgotten in life no matter how well they think they have done. The most important thing is for God not to forget you. What a great revelation!

If there is anything you must take away or learn from my story, this is it: your father, your mother or your brother may forsake you, but if God has not forsaken you, you have a future, and that future is bright. Many times we focus on people or things and miss out what God has planned for us. Don't put your trust in man or things but trust God to use people or circumstances to bring about your much-desired breakthrough. Don't work out how God is going to do it or totally leave Him out of the equation. He works with His agenda and timing for your life to achieve His purpose. Use your brain, but don't figure God out. The way of God is different from that of man. God will do whatever He would do anyhow, whichever way. The important thing is to have a clear perspective on that and to use discernment in the journey of life.

My experience has also taught me to appreciate what I have, and how to speak and react when others are going through diffi-culties. Never look down on anybody, unless you are helping them up. When I hear now that the devil has struck someone with cancer or a mystery illness, I don't try to work it out with my medical knowledge any more as I used to do; I spare a thought for them and pray that God ministers His peace and grace to them in their darkest hour. I pray that God bring them healing according to His promises for good health. When I hear now that someone has not made a job interview or lost their job, I don't flippantly say any more that they should practise better, try harder or simply get the right material. I simply pray that God should give them the strength to carry on and not give up and not deny Him. When I hear that a brother, a sister or a pastor has fallen into sin or messed up big time, or found themselves in big trouble, I don't say any more, "Why on Earth did he or she do that?" or that the person "should have known better" or "that serves him right". I realise that it is by the mercies and the grace of God that I have not been consumed by my own foolishness.

Anyone can be in a dark place in life and I now take time to say a prayer and have a thought for that person in difficulty. The more I do that, the more I realise that anyway, anyhow, God can bring anyone out of a dark situation as long as they are not looking in the wrong places.

11

God And Dark Places

In my study of darkness and people going through dark periods in their lives, I have established four truths about God and darkness. The first is that dark places are not new or strange to God – He created darkness in the first place. The second is that when you find darkness anywhere or a person in a dark situation, God is not far from there. In fact God is there. The third is that God has absolute control over darkness and uses it to fulfil His eternal purpose and agenda. The fourth is that God will make everything work together for good for you if you choose to allow him into your situation. God will use darkness in your life to glorify His name.

I cannot honestly tell you that I fully understand why some people face dark situations in their lives or why a good God would sometimes allow bad things to happen to good people and His own children. I have however come to realise that circumstances are part and parcel of life and of human existence. Why? I can't say. The Bible, in Ecclesiastes, puts it very poignantly: "But if a man lives many years And rejoices in them all, Yet let him remember the days of darkness, For they will be many. All that is coming is vanity" (Ecclesiastes 11:8).

The New John Gill Exposition of the Entire Bible explained Ecclesiastes 11:8 further this way: "though persons may live long, and enjoy much health and prosperity; yet, in the midst of all, they should consider, that it is possible that days of adversity and distress may come upon them." That is one of the most humbling statements I have read for many years. God has stated clearly in His words that we would face tribulations in this world. However, He has asked us to rejoice as He has overcome every adversity that might come our way. God chooses whatever situation we find ourselves in to glorify Himself. His plans are to make sure every-thing work out well for us in the end. When all is said and done, when the dust settles and when the music has faded, you are a winner.

Very early in the story of creation, darkness covered the face of the Earth and the spirit of God was moving upon the face of the waters (Genesis 1:2). You may ask "How on Earth could darkness be where the spirit of God was moving?" I have asked myself this question for many years – "What was God's spirit doing where darkness prevails?" I have come to realise that it is for His spirit to reign over darkness. Wherever you find darkness, God is right there; He is trying to sort out the mess and He will not allow darkness to prevail in your life.

God Himself created darkness and this is what Psalms 104:20 says: "You make darkness, and it is night, In which all the beasts of the forest creep about."

As if that was not convincing enough, God puts it this way in Isaiah 45:7: "I form the light and create darkness, I make peace and create calamity; I, the LORD, do all these *things.*"

Several verses of the Bible further confirm that darkness is not strange to God. In Exodus 20:21, Moses drew near onto the thick darkness where God was. In 1 Kings 8:12, the Lord Himself said He would dwell in thick darkness (cloud). Darkness and light are the same to God; He made them both, and according to His will and counsel, does whatever He likes with them. Because God made darkness, it cannot hide from God (Psalm 139:11–12). Everything is known to Him and that includes everything you are going through in the darkest period of your life. You cannot hide from Him and the problem cannot hide you from God. God is everywhere and He knows all things.

The Psalmist said he could not hide himself from God even

though he lays his bed in Hell (Psalm 139:8). Psalms 97:2 states that clouds and darkness are round about Him; and He made darkness His secret place. His canopy around Him was dark waters and thick clouds of the skies (Psalm 18:11).

God is the one that sets an end to darkness; He is the one who has the power to limit darkness in your life. 2 Samuel 22:10 reveals that God bows the heavens, and darkness was under His feet. God says in Isaiah 60:2 that even when darkness covers the Earth, His glory will arise upon you. When God starts to shine His light in your life, darkness will not be able to understand or withstand it (John 1:5).

When the sons of God went to present themselves to God in Job 1, Satan went also. God asked Satan: "Where have you come from?" Satan was so audacious in his reply: "From roaming through the Earth and going back and forth in it." Even the strongest of men would shiver hearing that! But God is not a man; He is God. Satan is a bad devil and wants to manifest and express his character everywhere he goes. He is the accuser of men and women. Satan is roaming to and fro in the Earth today – to destroy relationships, marriages, families, homes, societies and nations. The Earth does not belong to Satan; it belongs to God, but Satan is trying to possess it. His mission is to steal, to kill and to destroy. The evidence is all over the place – you only need to watch the news on your television, check the Internet or listen to the radio. Carnage and destruction are everywhere, but in all this, God is in control and would not allow evil to prevail no matter how bad the situation is. I will use Sally's story below to drive this message home.

Sally is a 33-year-old lady who ran away from home at the age of 14 – her parents were both alcoholics and did not know God. Sally's two younger brothers were later removed from their home to live with foster carers when the local social services thought their lives would be in danger. Sally joined her new "family" on the streets where she found love and acceptance, but she was soon drawn into a life of alcohol, drugs and prostitution. Sally was raped several times but she had no one to turn to – she relied on her company for her daily supply of heroin and crack cocaine. She was pressured into shoplifting and robbery and she later found herself in prison several miles away from home. Life became bleak and lonely; no one visited her in prison and no one cared.

Sally found God during her incarceration and became a born-again Christian. On returning to her local area after she left prison, she attended church a few times and started to train as a hairdresser. Sally kept her past to herself but soon started to crave for drugs and men. She fell through the net and started dabbling in drugs and prostitution to fund her habits. She injected practically all her limb veins with heroin and developed clots deep in her legs. And then the bad news – the right leg was rotten (gangrenous, black and swollen) and required amputation! Sally ended up in a wheelchair – she had not only lost her family, but a hairdressing career, her health and one of her legs. Life became tragically hopeless; you could call it a "valley of the dry bones" situation.

Let me give you a picture of what Ezekiel described in the "valley of the dry bones" (Ezekiel 37). You must notice two things: firstly, the bones were gathered in a valley, and secondly the bones were very dry. In geography, a valley is a low land surrounded by at least two hills. What that means for a person in a hopeless situation is that while they are trying to come out of a lowly place, a depression or a hole, other circumstances then surround them to keep them in. And that could be anything – war, famine, a natural disaster, a death in the family, a broken relationship, a financial crisis, illness or loss of a limb as in the case of Sally. Here is the account of the "valley of the dry bones":

> The hand of the LORD came upon me and brought me out in the Spirit of the LORD, and set me down in the midst of the valley; and it was full of bones. Then He caused me to pass by them all around, and behold, there were very many in the open valley; and indeed they were very dry. And He said to me, "Son

of man, can these bones live?" So I answered, "O Lord GOD, You know." Again He said to me, "Prophesy to these bones, and say to them, 'O dry bones, hear the word of the LORD! Thus says the Lord GOD to these bones: "Surely I will cause breath to enter into you, and you shall live. I will put sinews on you and bring flesh upon you, cover you with skin and put breath in you; and you shall live. Then you shall know that I am the LORD."'" So I prophesied as I was commanded; and as I prophesied, there was a noise, and suddenly a rattling; and the bones came together, bone to bone. Indeed, as I looked, the sinews and the flesh came upon them, and the skin covered them over; but there was no breath in them. Also He said to me, "Prophesy to the breath, prophesy, son of man, and say to the breath, 'Thus says the Lord GOD: "Come from the four winds, O breath, and breathe on these slain, that they may live."'" So I prophesied as He commanded me, and breath came into them, and they lived, and stood upon their feet, an exceedingly great army. (Ezekiel 37:1–10)

A valley with dry bones could be likened to a situation when for example, your bank manager finally decides to give you a business loan, and then your landlord gives you a quit notice to vacate the premises. Just as you found out that you are pregnant after years of barrenness, the doctor discovers fibroids in your womb – the fibroids are not just a few but everywhere. The fibroids are trying to abort the baby, and one is even blocking the passage through which the baby will come out. You are thanking God for your new job and three months later, your boss says he is struggling with the recession and cannot afford to keep the company afloat. You are being asked to leave work and there won't be any redundancy payment.

Someone in a "valley with dry bones" situation may have enrolled on a professional course, and while they are doing their final year project, the person develops a mental illness and can no longer read or concentrate. A "valley with dry bones" situation is when a person has used all their life savings to build a house and then an earthquake strikes. Homelessness beckons and nothing significant can be salvaged from the rubble. A farmer is in a valley full of dry bones when after planting his crops in season and waiting for harvest, floods come and washes everything away. A "valley with dry bones" situation could also be a challenging ministry, a failed business or troublesome marriage preventing or distracting you from reaching where you want to go.

Whether a dire situation is fibroids blocking the womb or trying to abort the baby, or the landlord giving a quit notice, an economic recession, a natural disaster or mental illness preventing someone from completing their final year project, these are mountains of opposition, and "valley with dry bones" experiences. Your situation may not be any of these, but if you have ever been hindered by seen or unseen forces, you will probably understand what I am trying to explain. Mountains are obstacles that want to prevent you from getting to your destination – you either get stuck behind them, go round or over them, or bulldoze them completely.

Secondly the bones in the valley which Ezekiel described were very dry indeed and unlike the bones you and I see every day. I once lived about two miles away from a local abattoir where cows were slaughtered for their meat. The workers removed the bones and put them in piles. The bone marrow and the bones' fat were removed to make fat products. Some of the bones ended up in poultry feeds but the majority were sold to merchants who burn, crush and grind them into powdery form before they are used locally or shipped abroad to make ceramic plates. These bones are turned into ornaments of beauty, designer food plates and kitchenware used by royals.

The bones described by Ezekiel in the Bible were completely different – they were very dry, completely useless and good for nothing. The bones were in damp, dark and dingy conditions in the valley; they couldn't be reached by light (light of the word of God), warmth from the sun (love of others) or fresh air (breath and spirit of God). The dry bones had been destroyed by dampness, feasted upon by termites, dented and decayed by the elements. There was no hope of recovery, the bones could not support anything and the slightest wind would blow them off in their powdery caricature state. You may think your "sorry and sad" situation is just like that but that is what God specialises in.

God asked Ezekiel: "Can these bones live?" Look at his reply: "O Lord GOD, You know." What an answer! I have heard some preachers knock Ezekiel and say he had little or no faith. I disagree. Ezekiel knew God as the Sovereign, and that God can do and undo, but I don't blame Ezekiel; the bones that Ezekiel saw were not like the ones I saw when I was growing up. The bones in the valley were very dry, completely useless and irrevocably hopeless. Ezekiel decided to play it safe – he concluded he had no clue about the situation, and referred God back to God. In today's language, Ezekiel would have said something like this: "God, I have never seen anything like this before; this is beyond my comprehension. You are the only one who has answers for a calamity such as this." God then said to him, "Ezekiel, these bones shall live". That is exactly what God is saying to the dry bones in your life.

God commanded the winds and there was a rattling noise and then bones joined onto bones. Tendons and flesh appeared on the bones, and skin later covered them. The bones came to life when the breath of God entered into them and they lived. You need to pay attention whenever there is a noise somewhere. The rattling noise in Ezekiel 37:7 is akin to the clarion call of God that says: "Come up hither; don't stay there in the valley; you're definitely coming out of darkness." The rattling of bones on bones is like the rumbling of the Holy Spirit breaking the shackles of bondage, and cutting the bars of limitation into pieces. The noise is also like the still small voice inside you saying: *"Beloved, you can make it. I have promised Myself that you will make it. As I did it for the bones in the valley, I will also do it for you. I will make a way out of the darkness."*

God will make a way where there seems to be no way. God will enlighten your darkness; impossible is not in His dictionary; and things that appear completely hopeless, He will turn around. This is His promise for you in Isaiah 42:16:

> I will bring the blind by a way they did not know; I will lead them in paths they have not known. I will make darkness light before them, And crooked places straight. These things I will do for them, And not forsake them.

12

A Way Out Of Darkness

I have seen God make a way out of darkness in very difficult situations. It doesn't matter how bad the situation looks. Jesus Himself went into the pit of Hell where eternal darkness reigns. Pandemonium broke out as Jesus descended into Hell; there was great rejoicing among principalities and powers. At last, the Son of man, who is the Son of God, had been delivered into their hands. Jesus overcame the principalities and powers in Hell; He made a show of them, and rose to a triumphant glory on the third day. A standard was thus set for you and me. You too can be triumphant.

The story of Sally in the last chapter was a case of dry bones in the valley, and a completely hopeless situation as described in Ezekiel 37. But that is exactly what God specialises in. Sally was cared for at a residential home for about nine months and was supported by her local social services. One day, Anne-Marie, a middle-aged nurse, was sent to her home to look after her, and to assist Sally with shopping. Anne-Marie took particular interest in Sally's plight, particularly after Sally told her she had also heard that her mother was dead and that her father was in prison for manslaughter.

Anne-Marie tried her best to comfort Sally, and she encouraged her and said: "Life can be hard, and sometimes you can't explain why some of these things happen. Just keep on thanking God." That seemed to set off fireworks! Sally barked, "Thank God for what? Are you a Christian?" Anne-Marie replied, "No, some of my friends are, and they seem sometimes not to bother too much about many things; they just keep on thanking God." Anne-Marie told Sally her friends attended a Christ's Temple church – she hadn't been there herself but her friends had invited her. Christ's Temple – that was the church Sally had attended a few times after she came out of prison before she lost her right leg.

Sally went back to Christ's Temple to re-dedicate her life to Christ – she had found God again. Actually, God had found Sally. She became more vibrant in her relationship with God; she preached to every support worker that cared for her at home. She became a youth leader at Christ's Temple, and many lives were won to God even while she was in her wheelchair. One day, Anne-Marie too decided to follow Sally to Christ's Temple. God can turn any situation around, no matter how dark. What a testimony!

I first watched the video of Nick Vujicic in my church – his life is another testimony of how God can turn an exceptionally hopeless situation around for His glory. Nick Vujicic was born to Christian parents on 4 December 1982 in Brisbane, Australia, without arms and legs. His father was a pastor at the time. There was no fore-warning and nothing prepared his parents for the ugly scene that met them the morning he was born. Up till now medical science has no explanation for his condition – a child that was completely well, save for the absence of all his limbs. His parents were devastated and understandably had concerns for his future.

When Nick Vujicic was old enough for school, the law did not allow him to be registered in a mainstream school, but with God's intervention and the determination of his parents, he became one of the first disabled students to be integrated into a mainstream school. You would have thought that with more understanding of Nick Vujicic's plight, life would be more bearable. That was not the case; he suffered from feelings of rejection and was bullied due to his disability. He became angry and depressed and thought about ending his own life.

I have seen and heard many people moan that life is hard; many of these moaners are jokers. I recently met a man who thought he was being attacked by the devil because the engine of his Mercedes Benz car knocked without any warning. I once spoke to a lady who thought her life was upside down because her childminder quit without giving notice. At a time in my life I also thought God had abandoned me because many of my classmates had travelled abroad and I couldn't do the same. How ridiculous can one get? Vujicic is a man who has no limbs; I mean all four limbs were missing. No word would be enough to describe the extent of his pain, his suffering and the obstacles that faced him. You could describe him as someone in the "valley of the dry bones".

Even in the most hopeless situation in which Nick Vujicic found himself, God was at work. With the support of his parents, Vujicic developed attitudes that saw him through the challenges he faced due to his severe disability and he refused to give up. He has travelled all over the world to offer inspiration to thousands of people. For a man with no limbs, Nick Vujicic has clocked more air miles than millions of able-bodied men and women; and more distances than many elite marathon runners the world has ever known. He has also written a best-seller entitled *No Arms, No Legs, No Worries!* He has a testimony and his life is counting for eternity. When I looked at Nick Vujicic's website recently, this is what he had written to thank his friends and admirers:

> Thank you for your wonderfully encouraging emails! They give me the much-needed strength I need to continuing doing what God has called me to do. I pray that you will always continue to seek God with your whole heart and never, ever give up on the purpose God has for you. With Love, Nick Vujicic.
> (www.lifewithoutlimbs.org)

With both his arms and legs missing, Nick Vujicic still believes God has called him on an assignment. That touched my heart. For Nick Vujicic, what the devil meant for evil, God turned around for good.

God will bring you out of dark places, and I have said "Amen" for you. Are you worried about your health today? God said you are already healed by His stripes – you just have to believe Him (Isaiah 53:5). He has promised to restore you to health and to heal your wounds (Jeremiah 30: 17). When you have fallen in a dark place, the eyes of God will locate you, His breath (spirit of God) will revive you, His life will strengthen you, His fingers will point you in the right direction, His mighty hands will hold you firmly strong and His presence will be with you. God will never leave you or forsake you even till the end of this age. Just put your trust in Him.

You may have sinned against Him but He is a forgiving God. He said in his word: "If My people who are called by My name will humble themselves, and pray and seek My face, and turn from their wicked ways, then I will hear from heaven, and will forgive their sin and heal their land" (2 Chronicles 7:14). God is saying His love for you is everlasting and that "I will build you up again and you shall be rebuilt" (Jeremiah 31:4). God wants you to know that in all things that have happened in your life "You are a conqueror and not a loser."

If your spouse, children or family have deserted you, or if you think that everything you have worked for all your life has vanished into thin air, this is what God promises you in His word:

> "Do not weep any longer, for I will reward you," says the LORD. "Your children will come back to you from the distant land of the enemy. There is hope for your future," says the LORD. "Your children will come again to their own land." (Jeremiah 31:16–17)

You may have been divorced, rejected or abandoned; or you may feel confused that your new life and existence seems very dark and unfamiliar to you. You may not even know which direction to go in or what step to take next. If that's you, this is what the Lord has promised you:

> I will bring the blind by a way they did not know; I will lead them in paths they have not known. I will make darkness light before them, And crooked places straight. These things I will do for them, And not forsake them. (Isaiah 42:16)

I want you to notice the word "will", used by God not once, not twice, but four times in that one single verse. "I will" is a powerful statement of intent and when God says "I will" do something, nothing on Earth or in Heaven can stop Him. You must burn that into your spirit.

You may have read something like this before and feel that despite waiting on God, nothing has changed in your life. You may even feel that despite the promises of victory, you are still being pursued by your adversaries. Don't be foolish in your thoughts – "The LORD will not allow the righteous soul to famish; But He casts away the desire of the wicked" (Proverbs 10:3). The hand of the Lord is not short to deliver, and nothing is too difficult for Him. When a man's way pleases God, He will make even his enemies be at peace with him (Proverbs 16: 7). When you have the word of God in your mouth, an unwavering faith in your heart and an assured hope in your view, believe me, just about anything can happen!

I can almost hear you say, "But God, you don't understand, my case is different." God is saying to you: *"I am the one yesterday, today and forever more. I am the unchanging changer; I change not. I change, change itself. If you trust me, even though your recent moves in marriage, business or finances have turned out to be mistakes, I will turn them into miracles. If you have been hitting and missing it, I will turn your floundering into flourish-ness. If you have messed up big time, I will turn your mess into a message. If your dreams have turned into nightmares, I, God, will turn them into visions. If you are being overwhelmed with life, I will turn your problems into promises. If the enemy has set a trap for you, I, God, will turn it into a triumph."* If you are being put under pressure by any situation in your life, God says, *"I will turn that into pleasure."* If you think you are a destitute today, God says *"I will change that situation and turn it into destiny for you."*

What is God going to do about the challenges you face today? You have asked a good question. God is saying to you: *"I am the Lord God Almighty; nothing is too difficult for me, I made the*

Heaven and the Earth. I hold everything in place with the strength of my right hand, and by the breath of my nostrils all things exist. Before me mountains melt like wax; I decide where the moon, the sun and the stars stay in the Heavens. I tell the sea where it should have its limits. I am God, I can do and undo. Put your trust in me."

Are you still in any doubt about what God can do? Please stay focused as you read on. In the next chapter, I want to encourage you with what God has done for others who came out of their dark places. I believe this will help you greatly. He did it for them and for me, and He will do it for you.

13

For Them, For Me And For You

The accounts of many people whom God has brought out of dark places cannot be contained in a single book. God came through for Isaac, for Jacob and his descendants. One minute Joseph was in prison, the next minute he was in the palace. God showed His mighty hand in the lives of the children of Israel who were held in captivity for over 400 years. As God was with Moses, He was with Joshua and with the judges – Samson, Deborah and Gideon. You have read about the works of Elijah and Elisha, and Samuel who anointed David king – God came through for all of them. The same was true for Jesus, Peter and Paul. You will now read about David, Jesus and ordinary men and women who came after them.

David, the son of Jesse

When David's breakthrough finally came, he ran from one dark cave to another, for his dear life, and from Saul who wanted to kill him. God brought him out. That did not spare David rejection by the Philistines with whom he initially encamped. The Amalekites raided David's camp and took away everything he and his men owned; wives, women and children. Ziklag was totally burnt down by the enemies. When David returned to Ziklag, his men who were in distress wanted to stone him. David did what a sensible man should do – he enquired of the Lord, and God told him to pursue the enemies to recover all that was stolen. David did and recovered all. The account is beautifully described in 1

Samuel 30:19: "And nothing of theirs was lacking, either small or great, sons or daughters, spoil or anything which they had taken from them; David recovered all."

Jesus Christ

Very few accounts would rival that of Jesus; a man whose predestined life was shrouded in mystery and darkness. Despite being born in a manger to a virgin mother, the plan of God did not change. Going to Egypt as a child could not truncate His future. Jesus was on the shelf for the better part of 33 years of His life; and when you expected Him to step out in style to thunderous applause for the grand finale, he was rejected by the people He came to save. Peter, His right-hand man denied Him three times; the disciples couldn't bear praying with Him in Gethsemane; His trusted treasurer Judas sold Him out to His captors. But the plans of God had to be fulfilled.

Jesus Christ encouraged the broken-hearted and the dejected; He asked God to forgive His tormentors; He pardoned the sins of the condemned. Jesus, the giver of life itself was mocked, ridiculed and beaten; He was spat at, struck and unceremoniously hung on the cross. Jesus later cried to the Father to spare Him the agony but God said: "No Son, My plan is working." As they nailed His hands and feet to the cross; as they tore His flesh and pierced His body, God kept on saying, "Yes, My plan is working; I can't deny Myself now; this thing has been predestined even before the foundation of the world. Even in all this agony and pain, I have promised Myself that You will make it, and that You will sit at My right hand." This mystery is clearly explained in the Bible as below:

> But we speak the wisdom of God in a mystery, the hidden wisdom which God ordained before the ages for our glory, which none of the rulers of this age knew; for had they known, they would not have crucified the Lord of glory. (1 Corinthians 2:7–8)

Even as Jesus was going through His pain and darkness, the plan of God was working. The rulers of this world crucified Him but God allowed it. Darkness fell upon the Earth and the veil that separated man from God was torn forever. Jesus was buried in a borrowed tomb; He went to Hell but triumphed on the third day. The principalities and powers could not hold Him bound and the salvation of mankind has been guaranteed forever. The plan of God came to pass despite all the challenges. The darkness in Jesus' life could not abort His destiny. In the same way, whatever you are going through now will not derail the plan of God for you.

Apostle Paul

Paul was a man who had been predestined right before the beginning of time to bring God's counsel to all mankind as we know it today. He was a man who was engulfed by more than one type of darkness in his life. First, it was the darkness of not knowing the true God, the Lord Almighty - Saul (later called Paul) went about persecuting Christians. Second, he became physically blind following his persecution of Christians but his eyesight was later restored. Third, Paul suffered many adversities-persecution, beatings and shipwreck but the darkness that was trying to envelop his destiny could not deter him. Paul was fiery for God and the things of God just as he was passionate when he was a sinner - that of course did not earn him many friends. Fourth, Paul ended up in jail on few occasions but that did not derail the purpose of God for his life.

The enemy thought he had figured Paul out and kept him in prison; and while he was there, he began to write many of the letters that have brought much insight into our understanding of God and life as we know it today. What the darkness in his life tried to abort, God turned around for good. Paul was in prison when he said, "I can do all things through Christ which strengthens me" (Philippians 4:13). He was in pains and chains behind iron gates in his darkest hours but he managed to write most of the two-thirds of the New Testament, the revolutionary epistles, which have been taught and researched the world over. Paul was put in darkness behind bars but he was a free man indeed.

Story of an unknown

During the Second World War, a US marine was separated from his unit on a Pacific island. The fighting had been intense, and in the smoke and the crossfire he had lost touch with his comrades. Alone in the jungle, he could hear enemy soldiers coming in his direction. Scrambling for cover, he found his way up a high ridge to several small caves in the rock. Quickly he crawled inside one of the caves. Although safe for the moment, he realised that once the enemy soldiers looking for him swept up the ridge, they would quickly search all the caves and he would be killed. That soldier was in the darkest moment of his life; worse still, in a cave!

As he waited, he prayed, "Lord, if it be your will, please protect me. Whatever your will though, I love you and trust you. Amen." After praying, he lay quietly listening to the enemy begin to draw close. He thought, *"Well, I guess the Lord isn't going to help me out of this one."* Then he saw a spider begin to build a web over the front of his cave. As he watched, listening to the enemy searching for him all the while, the spider layered strand after strand of web across the opening of the cave. *"Hah,"* he thought. *"What I need is a brick wall and what the Lord has sent me is a spider web. God does have a sense of humour."*

As the enemy drew closer, the US marine watched from the darkness of his hideout and could see them searching one cave after another. As they came to his, he got ready to make his last stand. To his amazement, however, after glancing in the direction of his cave, they moved on. Suddenly, he realised that with the spider web over the entrance, his cave looked as if no one had entered for quite a while. "Lord, forgive me," prayed the young man. "I had forgotten that in you a spider's web is stronger than a brick wall." God hides the miraculous inside the ridiculous; He uses the foolish things of the world to confound the wise. He is God.

Karoly Takacs, Olympian

Karoly Takacs served in the Hungarian Army in 1938 and was the top pistol shooter in the world. He had set his eyes on winning the gold medal in the 1940 Olympics, but unfortunately this dream came to an abrupt end: Takacs' right shooting arm was blown off in a serious accident after a grenade exploded in his hand during a military training exercise.

Takacs became depressed over the loss of his Olympic dreams. However Takacs did not give up and he learnt how to shoot with his left hand and practised by himself for several months. While he was doing this, he didn't tell anyone and secretly mastered the art of shooting with the only hand he had left.

Takacs later attended the Hungarian National Pistol Shooting Championship in the spring of 1939 where he met other competitors who were very sorry for him. They offered their condolences on the tragedy of the loss of his right hand but Takacs refused to join their pity party. He surprised them, and declared: "I didn't come to watch – I came to compete!" You can imagine the bewilderment and the doubt expressed on their faces. Takacs surprised everyone and won the competition! The Olympic Games did not take place in 1940 or 1944 because of the Second World War, but Takacs continued to train and won gold medals at both the 1948 and 1952 Olympic Games. God turned his tragedy into triumph.

Joni Eareckson Tada

At the age of 17 years, in the summer of 1967, Joni Eareckson Tada dived into a shallow lake while swimming with some friends. She broke her neck, and was paralysed from her neck down. Over a two-year period, she struggled with life, with her paralysis and with God. She was angry, bitter and depressed and her faith was shipwrecked. She even begged her friends to assist her to commit suicide. Joni searched for answers but none came, and then with the help of another teenage friend she began a process of healing. That accident was not because of a sin she had committed or a curse in her generation or family. God did not cause the accident either; that was the work of the devil. But the difficult question is: "Why did God allow such a horrible thing to happen?" I don't know.

In her story, Joni was certain that the devil was trying to destroy her dreams and make a mockery of her faith in God. She also knew that there is an all-wise, all-powerful and all-loving God who is able to turn a horrible situation into a positively good one and bring glory to Himself. Joni has been living in a wheelchair since her accident over forty years ago. She is open and honest about her struggles and limitations but she has also found herself in a deeper relationship with God. She has written over seventeen books and has travelled all over the world supporting the causes of people with disabilities. Although she is a quadriplegic, she is an internationally known mouth artist, talented vocalist, a radio host and an advocate for disabled people worldwide. Joni loves the Lord; God turned it around for her and He took the glory. This is how the Bible puts it: "And we know that all things work together for good to those who love God, to those who are the called according to *His* purpose" (Romans 8:28).

Mary Crowley

Mary Crowley is the sister-in-law of Mary Kay Ash, the make-up giant. Crowley founded Home Interiors & Gifts in 1957, but this was after she had been through a lot herself. Mary Crowley got married in 1932, had a son the following year, and a daughter in 1935 during the Great Depression. Without much help from her husband, she got a job to support her children and juggled being a mother with being the breadwinner for her family. Due to her personal inclination and Christian upbringing, she initially did not want to divorce her husband who was not assisting in any way. Eventually she did in 1939 and moved to Dallas, Texas with her two children.

At the beginning of the Second World War, Crowley was studying and also working full-time at an insurance company. She went through several struggles, and it is recorded that sometimes before pay day, she and her children had nothing to eat other than cereals and milk. When she couldn't sleep (as happened on many occasions) she would turn over her problems to God and say, "Lord, you know I've got to get my rest. You worry about these problems. You're going to be up all night anyway." And she found sleep.

Crowley attended a business school in Dallas and at the same time raised her children in a loving home. In 1948, Mary married David M. Crowley, Jr., someone she had met previously when she worked for the insurance company. While working as an account-ant for a furniture company, she met many women who wanted to make their house very attractive but who had little or no clue about what they wanted or how to choose fabrics or coordinate the colours. Crowley shared the same desire and soon a business idea was forming in her mind even without her knowing. As far as she was concerned, she wanted to help the customers, and God opened a door for her. A man who imported gifts and decorations later asked Crowley to become his sales manager in a new direct sales company. Things were fine for a while but after sales rocketed, the owner started to include cocktail parties into his company functions, something which Crowley objected to. Crowley had no choice other than to leave when the business owner allegedly put a limit on the maximum amount women sellers could make.

Crowley later started Home Interiors & Gifts in 1957 with the support of her husband. She hired many women who had previ-ously been totally dependent on their husbands, helped them work on their appearances and made them see who God really made them to be. Her daughter later opened the East Coast

Home Interiors and by 1962 the company recorded one million dollars in sales. Mary Crowley carried on working despite fighting two bouts of cancer. Before her death in 1986, she was invited to a conference with President Jimmy Carter, and she served on the board of directors of the Billy Graham Evangelistic Association. Of all that Mary Crowley related in her story, I consider this statement the most powerful: "God can mend any broken heart, provided you've given Him all of the pieces." The problem is that we choose not to give every piece to Him.

Mr Stuart Sharp

Mr Sharp, a 67-year-old man slept rough on the London streets for ten years. During that time he had a vision of a song he had composed 35 years before, after the death of his baby son, Ben. Mr Sharp had ended up homeless after separating from his wife and life became difficult and darkness descended. While on the street, he bought a guitar for fifty pence (half of one British pound) and taught himself music. Mr Sharp was drinking a bottle of whisky a night, and knew if he continued drinking that way, he would end up dead very quickly. Ten years is a very long time to sleep on streets which can sometimes be dark and very cold, and where the temperature can plummet below freezing point during winter.

While Mr Sharp was homeless, he met Anthony Wade, a musician, who offered him a place to stay and helped him transcribe his music. By 1994, Mr Sharp was rich and he bought a recording studio to realise his dream. He went on to be a millionaire through a career in sales and property and his music was later performed by at least ten international singers in the West End of London. God can bring destiny out of dark places. He did it for Mr Sharp and He can do the same for you.

Dave Dravecky

The story of Dave Dravecky will make you think again about life. Dravecky was riding high in his baseball career in 1988 and was looking forward to winning twenty games. Unfortunately a tumour developed in his left arm and half of his shoulder muscle had to be removed by surgery in October of that year. The doctor told him: "Outside a miracle you will never pitch again." Just under a year later, Dravecky stood on the mound and threw the first pitch of ninety-three pitches – he was still able to do what he used to do before the surgery. Dravecky was overwhelmed with his miraculous comeback and he couldn't stop talking about it. Then came a twist in the story – the darkness had returned.

Dravecky had to play another game five days later. He was very excited about his comeback and Dravecky went into the cage and threw a fastball. The next minute he was lying on the ground with a broken arm and was wheeled off. It was bad news, the cancer had come back! Dravecky wrote about going through a lot of difficult times, depression, struggles, pits and valleys. His wife became depressed too and he could not help her. Sadly, Dravecky later had his left arm amputated. But God turned an ugly situation around for Dave Dravecky and his wife Jan. They established Dave Dravecky's Outreach of Hope in 1991 to offer comfort, encouragement and hope to those who suffer from cancer, amputation or serious illness. Dave and Jan have written eight inspirational books and they currently publish *The Encourager*, a magazine on the emotional and spiritual aspects of suffering. This is what Dravecky said, in his own words:

> God causes all things to work together for good to those who love Him and are called according to His purpose. You know what? It's so that we might become more like Christ. What God does through the valleys of life is He shapes and moulds us into the image that He wants us to be. He gives us the strength to endure.

Dave Dravecky's life story is an interesting account of a man whose salvation was divinely orchestrated in his quest for success. He learnt through adversity that we can all need help at some point in our lives. It is important to be understanding and sensitive to others in need and it is okay to be honest and compassionate. Dravecky's story also teaches that it is okay to let people get help from others if we cannot help them, something he said he was reluctant to allow his wife to do initially. I was totally humbled by his account.

Daniel Carlock

Daniel Carlock, a 51-year-old aerospace engineer from Santa Monica, California developed post traumatic stress disorder and skin cancer from exposure after he was abandoned at sea, 12 miles off Long Beach in 2004. Carlock had joined a group of twenty scuba divers on an excursion in the Pacific Ocean. Shortly after entering the water with three dive buddies, Carlock developed some problems and was unable to equalise the pressure in his ears. That was tragedy in the making! He fell behind and tried to follow his partners' bubbles but he lost them. Carlock decided to end the dive after about fifteen minutes and he surfaced four hundred feet from their anchored boat. He tried to swim back to the boat but developed cramps in his legs. Despite blowing his safety whistle and waving a yellow inflatable diving sausage, no one on the boat saw him and nobody noticed he was gone. The boat moved away to escape strong currents and left Carlock to drift in the sea for five hours. Carlock was marked as being present on the boat, not once but twice. No one was looking for him – the boat crew only realised he was missing after three hours.

Carlock was lost at sea! At a point when Carlock was surrounded by thick fog in the Pacific, he recalled: "I had this feeling my spirit was getting ready to vacate my body." Although he tried to stay calm, he worried how his parents would react to the news of his death. Mr Carlock prayed, and said, "God I don't want to die and I want to be saved. I need your help." God answers prayers; you should be aware of this by now. Carlock was spotted by a boy scout who looked through his binoculars after seeing something floating in the water. A motor boat was sent to pluck him out from the sea – saved by God and the quick thinking of a small boy. Carlock was later awarded over one million pounds in damages six years after his ordeal.

Pastor (Mrs) Faith Oyedepo

I encourage you to read *Rescued from Destruction*, a very good book written by Pastor (Mrs) Faith Oyedepo, the wife of the man of God, Bishop David Oyedepo, the senior pastor of Winner's Chapel International. She revealed in her book how God snatched her from the jaw of death. Pastor (Mrs) Oyedepo, a disciplined woman, who had previously enjoyed good health, was preparing a bash to commemorate Bishop Oyedepo's 50th birthday in 2004 when the enemy struck. A tour of a few cities in the north of Nigeria and other international meetings had been lined up before "Shiloh", their annual meeting of the year at Canaan Land in Ota, Ogun State, Nigeria. Pastor Faith Oyedepo described in her account how she developed sudden pain in her arm, and how she endured the pains through the meetings before things got worse and she was unable to support herself. She was sustained by the word of God which she has embedded in her spirit since her teenage years. She was joined in her violent engagement with the power of darkness by her husband, Bishop Oyedepo and many servants of God who prayed with and for her. God is a faithful God; Mrs Oyedepo became well after about a year and returned to celebrate the goodness of God in the land of the living.

Susan Boyle

You may have heard about the 47-year-old Scottish spinster called Susan Boyle who was parachuted to international stardom recently. When she was young, Ms Boyle had dreamt of a singing career where she would make it big. She had a learning disability, possibly from brief oxygen deprivation at birth, but that did not stop her from dreaming. She was bullied in school and was teased by children in the locality where she lived. Often she was called different names, even as a grown-up.

Susan Boyle was left at home with her cat after her siblings left home one by one and she had the task of looking after her ageing mother who died at the age of 91. She only worked as a trainee cook for about six months but she would regularly offer help to the elderly and did some voluntary work. As time went by, Susan Boyle's dream of making it big as a singer appeared to have eluded her. She sang at various places without achieving the breakthrough she had always wanted. She found it difficult to sing for a period of time because of the upset caused by her mother's death. But there lay ahead of her destiny hidden in the dark places of her life.

On Saturday 11 April 2009, Susan Boyle attended the *Britain's Got Talent* show in Glasgow, Scotland. The nation and others watching from across the world were greeted by a moderately built lady with unkempt greying hair, a frumpy look and an eccentric demeanour. Everyone was bemused given the look on the faces of the audience. Many people including me (I must confess) weren't expecting her to do well at all. Susan Boyle was nervous and her Scottish accent didn't help either. She fitted the stereotype perfectly. I remember telling my children that TV producers usually look for clowns to bring to shows in order to keep the atmosphere lively and to spice things up. I have never been so wrong.

When Susan Boyle said "I'm trying to become a professional singer", everyone laughed. And then her turn to sing came. The audience was shocked and the atmosphere changed in an instant after Susan Boyle sang "I Dreamed A Dream" from *Les Miserables*. Susan Boyle did not have the appearance of an A-list celebrity but she had the voice of an angel – something which the darkness in her life had tried to overshadow. Her performance was described as the "biggest surprise", "stunning" and "amazing" by the three judges. She got "Yes" from all the judges and she continued on the show.

It didn't take long before Susan Boyle's name was plastered all over newspapers and the Internet worldwide – a clip of her audition at one point received over 50 million hits. Offers started pouring in and she was wanted on the Oprah Winfrey Show. With her new-found fame and the unending attention she received, Susan Boyle crashed under enormous pressure and was admitted to a psychiatric hospital for stress. She bounced back to continue on the show and she went on to win second place. She later appeared on Larry King Live on CNN with Piers Morgan and she became a global phenomenon.

Susan Boyle, a woman whose circumstances of life and darkness had hidden in a council house for decades, became someone with international appeal and acclaim. According to Wikipedia, the online encyclopaedia which has a page for her, Susan Boyle was officially recognised by Guinness World Records in September 2010 as having had the fastest-selling debut album by a female artist in the UK, the most successful first-week sales of a debut album in the UK, and was also awarded the record for being the oldest person to reach number one with a debut album in the UK. That can only be God.

Me

My dark places were nothing compared to the stories you have just read, but Jesus did it for me. God pulled me out of the miry clay and put my feet on solid ground. He was there through thick and thin. When death took away my 'defences', Jesus said: *"I will not leave or forsake you even till the end of age."* When I was sick and tired, He healed me and gave me strength. When I was lonely and confused, He kept me company and gave me directions. When I thought I had been abandoned in a foreign land, he made me an ambassador to declare His glory. When it was very dark, He shone His countenance upon my life and lit my path. My testimony today is that He is my hiding place; He has protected me from trouble and has surrounded me with songs of deliverance (Psalm 32:7).

You

Yes, you! If Jesus could do it for me, He can do it for you also. Yes He can! The fact that you are reading this book now means that God has brought you this far, and He doesn't do half-measures nor start a thing and not finish. The God that was in Joseph and David is not different from the one living inside you now if you have accepted Christ as your Lord and Saviour. What you do in the time of adversity depends on what you do with the God that is inside you. If you tap into the power of God inside you today, He will turn your darkness into destiny. If you call upon Him today, He will turn your mourning into dancing and your sorrow into gladness.

People might think it's all over for you but God says: *"No, with Me nothing is over until I say so."* Yours is to believe, leave the workings to God. You must not figure Him out; God doesn't think or act like man, His ways are different (Isaiah 55:8) but sure. God is not a man; and it is impossible for Him to lie. He has determined before time began that His thoughts towards you will always be good, irrespective of what the devil wants to do. God will use everything for His glory, and you are coming out of dark places.

The Chilean miners

You mustn't forget about the 33 Chilean miners. The activities to rescue the miners came to a head at 03:51am GMT on 13 October, when the first rescued miner entered the shuttle. Many of them prayed that God should spare their lives and prayers were offered for them all around the world. God stayed with the miners, and He spoke to several of them: *"I knew all about this even before you were trapped; I am everywhere, and I am here to keep you company. I will not leave you or forsake you even after all of you have come out of this hell hole."*

God is not one to waste any experience; the trapped miners were already discussing how to sell their story, and each of them could possibly earn up to £300,000 from film roles, or a staggering £10,000,000 from what was supposed to be a disaster. I was glued to the television as the miners were plucked out one by one. Then the leader of the rescue team, Manuel Gonzalez, switched off the light in the mine as he made his way up the shuttle. When Gonzalez finally surfaced, the whole world gave thunderous applause. An era of darkness in the lives of the miners was shut out forever!

It was great that all the 33 miners and their rescuers came out alive, and brilliant that their lives would never be the same again; however that was not the greatest testimony. The greatest testimony was that God used that dark period in their lives to glorify His name, and He did it in style, in front of TV cameras, and the whole world. God's name was plastered all over newspapers everywhere and several miners acknowledged His mighty hands in their breakthrough. One of the miners stepped out of the shuttle, knelt down, and declared, "I was with God and with the devil. And I reached out for God." Do you feel trapped today? My friend, reach out to God.

14

Now That You Are Out

Darkness may be allowed to operate in your life, but only for a season – after that, it must give way; and light must come. Your problem has an expiry date, and what's more, in God's calendar, the day never ends with the night – it's always the other way round. So, whatever night you are experiencing right now, be assured, it is passing quicker than you think – and joy comes in the morning. In the morning, everything becomes clear, the dark clouds clear away; the shadows are all gone; the cold of the night gives way to the warmth of the light. There is no more need to weep; the enemy cannot surprise you anymore; the unknown cannot threaten you anymore; the process cannot frighten you anymore and the pressure cannot crush you anymore. And you are no longer afraid of the dark – the night no longer scares you, because you've already been through it.

The above is an excerpt from the sermon notes of the message preached by Dr Tayo Adeyemi, Senior Pastor, New Wine Church, London on Easter Sunday morning in March 2005. You may be going through a dark period right now or on your way out. You might even have been through darkness but now you are out. The only way is out and you are coming out!

Praise Him

Praise Him, praise Him, and praise Him. You will praise Him when you find yourself in dark places if you believe God is able to see you through. If you have lost hope of making it, praise will not mean anything to you. God has already concluded in His book that you are coming out – it cannot be reversed. He is God and does not change; the rest is down to you. Praise Him when you are on your way out and praise Him when you are finally out. What can you offer to God apart from your praises? What can you give to a God that already owns everything? If all the hairs on your head became tongues, they are never going to be enough to express gratitude to God. Just give Him praise.

Magnify the Lord at all times; His praises should never cease from your mouth. Today I will sing my "Song of Ascent" like David did in Psalm 124:1-3:

> "If it had not been the LORD who was on our side," Let Israel now say – "If it had not been the LORD who was on our side, When men rose up against us, Then they would have swallowed us alive, When their wrath was kindled against us."

Anyone who understands what God has done for them would be broken and very thankful. Basically what David was saying in Psalm 124 was that, left to men, life and circumstances, our lives would have been consumed; and the enemy would have taken us for supper. But God did not allow it. I will sing another song of David as in Psalm 103:1-5 but this time I have decided to personalise it:

> Bless the LORD, O my soul; And all that is within me, *bless* His holy name! Bless the LORD, O my soul, And forget not all His benefits: Who forgives all *my* iniquities, Who heals all *my* diseases, Who redeems *my* life from destruction, Who crowns *me* with lovingkindness and tender mercies, Who satisfies *my* mouth with good things, So that *my* youth is renewed like the eagle's.

Strengthen others

The second thing you should do when you are out of darkness is to strengthen others. You can do this in four ways – by being understanding of people in difficult situations, by the words of your mouth, by your good acts, and by your testimony. Peter was a man who went through dark periods in his life. He was called from his fisherman's lifestyle into ministry and was one of Jesus' lieutenants. He was so committed he was keen to go to prison with Jesus and to die for Him. However when life became hard, Peter couldn't even pray with Jesus for one hour. Peter was sorrowful and was disappointed with himself after he denied Jesus, not once but three times. Eventually when Jesus his master was unceremoniously hung on the cross, he lost his defence, his moral and spiritual compass. When Peter thought it was all over, he went back to his fishing business. Thank God, Jesus did not declare that it was all over for him. He had already prayed for him: "But I have prayed for you, that your faith should not fail; and when you have returned to Me, strengthen your brethren" (Luke 22:31–33).

Jesus is always praying for you and had done so for Peter as he knew what was going to happen. The world may have ruled you out and think it's all over but it's not over until God says so. When you are out, strengthen others who are going through their dark places. God will not let your experience go to waste; He will glorify Himself in all situations.

Understanding

I am not suggesting that you join someone in a pity party but empathise with others; put yourself in their shoes, and consider how you would have felt if you were the one going through difficulties. Refrain from making silly statements like Job's friends; say only words that will build people up and not words that would tear people down or tear them apart. Encourage others and strengthen them in your prayers and in practical ways. Sometimes experience can teach a person to be humble but you don't have to go through a bad experience to learn how to act sensibly and sensitively towards someone in trouble. We can all use our holy hands to wipe others' dirty feet; we can all show someone the way, and we can all wipe away the tears from the eyes of those who are hurting. This is the message of the kingdom but it takes understanding and wisdom to know that.

Practical actions

A gentleman who used to attend my church several years ago had found himself in the throes of addiction and dependence on alcohol. As a mental health professional, I wanted to understand his difficulties, and I referred him to the local addiction services and solicited for help and treatment from his doctor. I assisted him financially and prayed for and with him. I became aware that he was living in squalor and in a degenerate condition – one day I went to his flat with my wife and we took clean clothes, soap and disinfectant with us. Although we were met with a horrible sight, we rolled up our sleeves, cleaned up the house and cleared out the mess over three days. We soiled our holy hands to clean his dirty feet. The gentleman was restored into a clean environment to begin to piece his life together once again. We had made the song "Lord, I am Available to You" real in our lives and in the gentleman's life. To God be the glory.

Give your testimony

People may want to belittle your experience and want to explain your miracle away – I would advise you not to get into any complicated argument with anyone. When Jesus Christ healed the blind man, people asked the question, "Is this the man who could not see before; how did it happen?" He did not explain to them whether it was his eyelashes, cornea or retina that received healing; the man simply said, "As far as I am aware, I was blind before, now I can see. How it happened I can't tell you, but the evidence is clear for you to see." Religious, philosophical or academic argument profits no one – don't ever get into it. Give your testimony; talk about the goodness of God in your life; talk about what He has done for you, and give glory to your Father in Heaven.

Be productive

When Joseph came out of his predicament in the land of Egypt he named his first son Manasseh, and the second, Ephraim. The two names – *Manasseh*: "For God has made me forget all my toil and all my father's house" and *Ephraim*: "For God has caused me to be fruitful in the land of my affliction" are linked and it was not coincidence. Joseph knew God had brought him out of dark places, and rather than plotting revenge against all the people who had offended him, he chose to forget his sufferings and continued to be productive. Talk to other people about Christ and the mercy of God. Avail yourself of every opportunity to talk about the salvation of Christ to the people you meet. I know many people who came to know the Lord when they were going through a crisis in their life. No matter how bad a situation might be, it is a tool in the hand of God.

Enjoy life to the full

Abundance and full life are the promises of God for you – enjoy them and don't let anything hold you back. You have won one battle, but another might come – to take you from glory to glory. One of the many things I plan to do in the near future is to visit Dublin, this time with my family. I am looking forward to enjoying that moment, and visiting Avalon House, the bed and breakfast hostel where I stayed a night on my arrival; South Circular Road in Dublin 2, the ferry port and the bus station in the city centre. I would however make sure that the red bag doesn't go with us. Red bag or no red bag, the *Gardai* would be friends with us as there is nothing to fear any more.

I am definitely out of darkness, although there are still many other things that I am asking God to do in my life. I have however decided to wait for and on God as He is the only one who has the answers. I once listened to a message called "Celebrate While You Are Waiting." I found that out to be true – you can wait and celebrate at the same time. Why not enjoy the moment? "Life isn't about how to survive the storm, but how to dance in the rain" (Taylor Swift). You are definitely coming out of dark places. You can dance and you can sing; and as you do, you will arise in Jesus' Name!

To God be all the glory, honour and praises forever and ever. Amen.